# The Unfiltered Guide
# to
# Medical Office Management

By Don Self

# The Unfiltered Guide to Medical Office Management

First edition copyright ©2010 Don Self

Library of Congress Catalog Number Pending

Published by *The Unfiltered Press*, Whitehouse, Texas

Cover Design and layout by Joe Self

Printed in the United States of America

ISBN: 97 80982718704

# Acknowledgements

The problem with making a list of people you want to express thanks to is that you invariably will miss someone. I know where to start, and that is in thanking God for not only sending His son to pay the ultimate price for me, but also for giving me a wonderful set of parents, good health, a loving & supportive wife and family & friends, and the chance to live in America. I'll talk more about Jeff Marsh later, but if it had not been for Jeff, I would not be in the medical field today, so thanks goes to he and Rosemary for taking a chance on me back in 1984.

Another person that has been influential dating back to the mid 80s in my career is Terry McVey who owns McVey Associates, Inc. coding, collection and reimbursement seminars. Prior to leaving Jeff, I called and asked Terry if he thought the country could use another reimbursement consultant and he encouraged me and is largely responsible for the guarantee that I've always given in my consulting. Others that have had a positive impact on my success include my father, Polly Dunlap, Rick Benson, Ray Cathey, Laureen Jandroep, Greg Schnitzer, Fred Wolfe, Quin Buechner, Barbara Cobuzzi, John Bishop, Todd Thomas, John Jackson, Cyndee Weston, Seth Canterbury, Charlene Burgett, Frank Cohen, Jin Zhou and definitely not least are my business partners, Keith & Julia LaBonte.

About 3 ½ years ago, Keith and I started working together and since then, we have helped hundreds of primary care physicians improve their patient care, obtain better results with their patients and increase their income dramatically (in most cases).

Finally, thanks to my wife Angie for understanding why I drag myself into bed at 1:30am so many nights after writing for hours on this book. She, like my parents has always supported and had faith in whatever venture I was delving into (except the multi-level things) Thank you to the thousands of physicians, office managers, coders, billers and staff that have attended my workshops, seminars and restrained themselves from throwing rotten fruit at me. My appreciation also goes to Laura A. Talbert, CPC, for the best name idea for this book, but while I am politically incorrect, that name is trademarked, so I adopted the Unfiltered Guide.

## Endorsements:

After 17 years of practice I felt I had a reasonably efficient well-run practice. I still at times found myself discouraged by cash flow issues, which I found to be a fairly common problem among primary care practices in today's medical climate. Over the years I have heard many promises from many consultants, and I was more than a little skeptical when you were recommended to me.

Don, I must tell you that it was very refreshing when I quickly realized that you were not just another salesman with pie in the sky ideas. Your analysis of my practice was thorough and extremely accurate. Incorporation of some of your most basic suggestions immediately impacted my bottom line, but what was most impressive was the fact that you focused your recommendations not on money but on enhanced patient care.

As I have continued to incorporate your ideas, I have seen a substantial improvement in the overall financial health of my practice. As you know, some of your ideas will still take several months to fully implement, but I have great confidence that my ability to care for my patients will only continue to improve.

More than anything, I have come to think of you more as a friend than as a consultant. Your core belief that by doing the right thing for the patient will result in the money taking care of itself has proven to be quite true. Thanks for your continued concern for me and my practice and I look forward to a long and fruitful relationship.

A.H. Tilley, MD    Pinnacle Physicians Group, Malvern, Arkansas

---

I am a solo practice primary care/sports medicine provider in Missouri City, Texas. I have been using Don and the ANSAR testing equipment in my office since August of 2007. During that time, I have identified at least two patients with severe autonomic neuropathy requiring urgent cardiology evaluation. In both of those cases, the cardiologic evaluation confirmed severe coronary disease and prompted change in medical management. In many other cases, I have been able to manipulate hypertension medication changes compatible with autonomic state and coming up with better control.

This added service has increased my ability to provide quality care for my patients with objective data. The fact that this study is non-invasive and takes less than 20 minutes to complete makes it very acceptable to my patient base.

---

I highly recommend the implementation of Don's suggestions in any primary care office. Thank you for providing me with the opportunity to spread the news. David Braunreiter, MD    Missouri City, TX

Economic survival and effective, timely, and affordable healthcare delivery in an increasingly complex and tumultuous healthcare market necessitates that Osteopathic Physicians continuously implement proactive rather than reactive clinical and practice management systems. For more than 20 years Don Self & Associates has helped pave Community Medical Clinic's roadmap to success through informative state and national workshops, monthly newsletters, timely legislative and coding alerts, practice site and management systems evaluations and solutions. Don's recommendations on implementing new diagnostic technologies, laboratory testing methodologies and invaluable advice on dealing with onerous insurance policies have enabled our family practice clinic not only to survive, but thrive in its operational, financial and clinical health outcomes and most importantly in improved doctor-patient outcomes.    Hector Lopez DO El Paso, TX

I was very impressed when I first heard Don speak at the AOA convention in Anaheim, and I subsequently purchased the Ansar and PFT machines. He took good care of me and I am providing even better care for my patients because of him, not to mention the satisfaction of increased reimbursements.    Ernesto Quinto, D.O Sacramento, CA

You have helped me in so many ways. Your recommendations have allowed me to diagnose and treat my patients for autonomic conditions that would otherwise have gone undetected. I just diagnosed 2 patients last week with atrial fibrillation. You also have helped me with billing and coding. I have learned the correct way to get reimbursed for all that I do with my patients. You have encouraged me to use my osteopathic skills and use them to ease painful musculoskeletal conditions for my patients. I have increased revenue and I have been able to sustain a fully staffed office as a solo practitioner even in these tough economic times. A patient of mine had been suffering with "IBS" for 10 years. Thanks to you, we found she was intolerant to fructose. She was eating a granola bar and yogurt every morning both of which had fructose added to them. She changed the brands she was buying and now she is symptom free. So you have helped me in many ways. But even more, you have helped me help others get the medical intervention they need to be healthy and well. And that is why I do what I do. I love what I do. And thanks to you I will continue to make a difference in my patient's lives.     Tasha   Wallace, D.O.          Lehigh Acres, FL

---

Having known you for many years and thinking I never "needed" your services I attended a lecture you gave and what heard made me feel like I was falling behind in my approach to managing my office.    After a visit to my office and implementation of a few suggestions, within 6 months I had realized over a 30% increase in office revenue which has allowed me to add new employees and more diagnostic equipment which will continue to increase my office bottom line.
Jeffrey Lindenbaum, D.O.   Yardley, PA

A little more than 3 years ago, we met in your seminar and since then, we have been following your advice. You have always willingly answered our questions and helped us with billing and ancillary services. We have told others how much you have helped us and in the almost 3 years since we have been using your recommendations, we have increased our annual income by more than $200,000 a year. Last year, you introduced us to the ANSAR and although we do bone density scans, PFTs, EKGs, NCVs and other services, none of them even come close to the ANSAR as far as reimbursement and patient care goes.

J Michael Holder, D.O., LTD        Phoenix, AZ

---

We're doing great. Praise the Lord! " I am sooooooo very glad that we finally opened our eyes and agreed to follow your recommendations for our practice. Our patients have benefitted clinically and our practice income has seen a dramatic increase in the years we've been adopting your suggestions."

Cindy & Michael Benavides, D.O.     Dallas, Texas

---

This information is fantastic. It's exactly what office managers and physician's need to read and hear in these troubling economic and litigious times. Proper reimbursement has become the most difficult task for every physician's practice. Way to go Don!"

John Bishop, P.A.

This book is the fasttrack to moneytown. You've done what I've wanted to write about for years.
Steve Verno

Don regularly contributes helpful information to the medical billing industry and I suspect that as long as he is around, we will continue to learn from him.        Cyndee Weston, Executive Director, American Medical Billing Association

Along with their diploma, this book should be given to all medical school graduates. I only wish we had this type of practical information available when my husband started his practice!
Marvel J Hammer RN CPC CCS-P PCS ACS-PM CHCO MJH Consulting

I know Don Self personally and professionally. Any advice and direction he has given me has always been RIGHT ON THE MONEY.    Lee Browder,  National Director, PAHCS

"Complete practice management, authoritative and experienced writings are difficult to come by. Don's book is one that qualifies. All in healthcare management should read it."    Terry McVey, President, McVey Associates, Inc.

*"The Unfiltered Guide To Medical Office Management"* written by Don Self will keep you interested, give you knowledge and make you laugh at the same time. I have read many practice management books over the past 9 years and this book is a keeper. I would advise any practice manager to make this small investment for their career.

Desiree R. Baylin, CMOM, CPM-HRS    Exec. Dir. Physician Office Managers Association of America (POMAA)

This book is dedicated to my mom, Patricia Anne Nolen Self (1937 – 2006) who, along with my father JW, taught me to never let circumstances or doubts or others convince me that I cannot achieve everything that I desire to do. There isn't a day that goes by that I don't miss                                                                    her.

# Introduction

The year was 1859 and the preacher & his covered wagon arrived in Early, Texas and asked the proprietor of the Mercantile store where the town usually had revival meetings. He was told "about 2 miles north of town, there is a level place owned by old man Moize and he allows it". So, the preacher put up his handwritten signs around town, proclaiming a "Revival will be held at 7pm on Saturday – 2 miles north", and then he headed north to set up his revival tent. Come Saturday at 7pm, only one lone cow hand rode up on his horse, tied him up outside the tent, walked in and sat on the front bench.

The preacher stood behind his makeshift podium, on the planks of wood that elevated him about 18 inches in the air and told the cowboy: "I've been preachin for nigh onto 12 years and always had a full tent at every meetin and tonight, you're the only one that showed up and I'm not that sure of what to do"

The cowboy sitting there thinks a minute and says in a slow Texas drawl "Wa'll, it seems to be that if I went out to feed my cattle with a wagon full of feed, and only one cow showed up – I'd feed that one cow".

That made sense to the preacher, so he spent the next 60 minutes teaching a hail and brimstone sermon covering all of the points of the gospel and salvation and didn't leave anything out, and at the end – he asked the cowboy what he thought.

The cowboy took another minute before answering and said "Well, I'm not booklearned and I ain't all that smart, but it seems to me that if I had gone out to feed my cattle and only one showed up, I'd feed that one – but I wouldn't dump the whole load on that one!"

By the time you finish this book, you may feel like I dumped the whole load on you as we have a lot to cover in this book.  I also decided that it is only the first of several books that will be titled "Don's Unfiltered Guide to..."

Let me also warn you that I do not ascribe to the politically correct ideologies that are typically found in Harvard, Hollywood or the Hamptons, and the politically incorrect term has been trademarked, so my books will be "unfiltered".   So, therefore, if I offend the elite or those who believe that you have to continue doing things the way you have been doing it for 30 years because you HAVE been doing that way for 30 years – so be it.   If you belong to the Clinton or Obama crowd that believes that physicians should NOT be allowed to make a profit – you don't want to read this book.  If you believe that a nationally mandated healthcare system, overseen by the federal government and a czar appointed by the President is the only thing that will save our country, please do not buy this book.  If you hope to find ways to commit fraud or to legally or illegally get insurance carriers to pay you money for services you should not be paid for – don't waste your time on this book.   Oh yeah – if you get offended by people referencing the Bible or Jesus or Christianity – then you surely SHOULD buy this book as it sounds like you need some old fashioned honesty.

This book is designed to help you stay legal and to ethically be paid what you should be paid for the services your physician and providers are rendering. It will not help you commit fraud and my personal philosophy is that if you're willfully committing fraud, I will do all I can to help you change your attire to an orange jumpsuit. It has been my pleasure to work with the O.I.G. and Medicare to get crooked businesses and crooked physicians penalized and I'll continue to do so — so keep it honest or find a different consultant to help you.

It's been my honor to consult with physicians since about 1984, thanks to the Lord, my wife and my close friend Jeff Marsh. I started out in mid 1984 working for Jeff with physicians and their accounts receivable. If you've been in this business for awhile, you may remember the superbills, ledger cards, day sheets and pegboard system (also called the One-Write system from Control-o-fax).

Jeff hired me to sell those to physicians and dentists (don't ever make the same mistake I made once of saying "doctors and dentists" because dentists ARE doctors) and we would be asked to make sure the coding on the superbill was correct. Before long, I was doing more consulting than I was selling forms and the consulting part was free, so in October of 1987, I gave Jeff a 3 month notice and on January 1st of 1988, I went to work as a full time reimbursement consultant.

OK – full time wasn't exactly accurate, as my day consisted of visiting physician offices on cold-calls handing out business cards during office hours and painting house numbers on curbs in the evenings, teaching medical office management classes at the junior college in Tyler 2 nights a week and serving in the U.S. Naval Reserve in Dallas once a month to support Angie and our 3 young sons.

The Lord blessed my efforts, so it was less than a year later that I was able to give up all of the side jobs and concentrate solely on reimbursement consulting and that led to me writing a book 22 years later.

As a consultant, my guarantee to clients is simple. If we cannot help them increase their annual income by at least $100,000.00 per year – legally and ethically - they do not pay us for our consulting. It's really not that difficult to do, since we only offer this to primary care physicians (specifically Family Practice, Internal Medicine & Geriatrics).

I can imagine that it might be more difficult to do with certain specialties, such as Chiropractors, Dermatologists, Allergists, surgeons, etc..., but the reason it is so simple for us to accomplish with primary care is that they have so many opportunities for improvement. Not only are they expected to perform a considerable amount of diagnostics (EKGs, breathing tests, peripheral arterial testing, heart rate variability testing, gastrointestinal testing, bone-density, etc), but they also have a phenomenal opportunity for us to help them in the areas of clinical lab testing and especially in the areas of coding.

It is very rare that we come across a Family Practice or Internal Medicine practice that they are performing the clinical lab that they should be and it is even rarer that we find those offices astute enough to be doing them in their own office.

That, combined with the fact that most primary care physicians routinely under-code, mis-code and NOT code for many of the services they provide. Many clinics still have office processes that are hurting their ability to collect what they should — which makes our goal of identifying how to increase their income much easier to accomplish.

One way that we do NOT recommend physicians attempt to increase their annual income is by making them work more hours than a normal 40 hour work week. I happen to believe that God prefers our priorities to be God first, spouse second, children third and work 4th. You'll notice that I did not say "family second" because I've seen too many younger people get the spouse and children priority mixed up — but that is a whole nother book! (Yes — I may be making your spell checker very nervous — but this is how I talk). Anyway — I dearly wish that I had lived by those priorities more in my own life, although I have tried hard to be there for my family, but it's easier to play Monday morning quarterback as we look back at 30 years of our life.

We hope to show you in this book how to work smarter and not harder or longer. If you're a parent — you NEED to be home at night for your spouse and kids.

They will grow up with you or without you and when they are gone – it will be YOU that missed out (as well as them) – but it will be you that will be spending the rest of your life wishing you had been there for more school activities, to help them with homework, to watch them play little league, etc...   It IS possible for you to increase your income by working smarter and still make it home in time for dinner every night, as attested to by some physicians who have listened to and followed our advice.

So – this book is going to give you tips and ideas.  For 21 years, I've been writing a monthly 8 page newsletter that is sent to subscribers only and many of the ideas in this book have been covered in my newsletters several times and some have not made it to the newsletters....yet.

Since I will reference some CPT codes and modifiers at times in this book, we want to thank the AMA for allowing us to use them under fair-use, so we are adding the following here and at the end of the book:

"CPT copyright 2010 American Medical Association. All rights reserved.  CPT is a registered trademark of the American Medical Association."

# Office Policies

## Location:

Prior to opening the doors of your practice, you should weigh several decisions carefully, after doing due diligence on the subjects we'll discuss. Most physicians will make the decision as to where to locate the practice without seeking counsel from existing physicians in the area, and that may not be the best idea.

If you're thinking of the placement of your own clinic, then it makes sense to do some homework and ask some of the other physicians in the area for their advice. Most physicians do not approach the concept of competing practices the same way that auto dealers or auto sales companies do (they do not want competition). Many are looking for someone to refer to or someone to share call with or someone to take part of the nursing home business or emergency room duties. You do not usually see this in the auto sales arena — but you definitely see it in the medical office family. They may know of a physician getting ready to retire or perhaps even looking for someone to mentor for a year or two before handing them the keys to a viable practice. You also want to ask whether the other physicians in the area are taking new patients, how long it takes to get an appointment as a new or established patient, whether they accept Medicare or Medicaid, etc...

As unbelievable as it may sound, there are many primary care practices that are not accepting Medicare, simply because someone has misled their physician into believing that it is a good business move to limit or exclude Medicare patients.

That is not the case in 99% of primary care offices – yet we're finding more and more that are excluding the Medicare population.

In my opinion, you'll make more money from a Medicare patient than you will any other type of patient, if you are in primary care –

- IF you AND your staff are doing a good job of knowing what services to render, how to bill for it and how to document it properly, and
- IF you're providing **GOOD** medical care instead of mediocre care.

We'll get into that much more in later topics, but the lesson is that you need to do your homework before determining where you will locate your practice.

One good place may be where the other primary care physicians are foolish enough to be turning away Medicare patients, so that you may have ample referrals to get your practice busy at a faster rate than otherwise.

## Marketing your practice

There are probably a dozen books on the market today about how to market your practice and many of them have great ideas. Personally, I'm not crazy about advertising in the paper or on the radio or even on television stations (including on Cable channel 1 that runs nothing but printed ads in some markets). Other than word of mouth (which seems to be the best), I prefer two venues of marketing:

## Column In Local Newspaper:

It seems that most newspapers are looking for weekly or monthly columns that discuss healthcare, preventive healthcare, diabetes, hypertension, nutrition, etc... and they are willing to run these for free. They may not be willing to pay you – but your real pay comes from the exposure to people in your community that will see you as a resource and that is where you'll get a lot of new patients. Contact a few local publications and ask them if they would like a regular column from you on issues that affects their readers.

Then you sit down and write a few columns about allergies, how to take care of diabetes, how dangerous it is to be dehydrated and what causes it, how sleep apnea not only is indicative of stress, depression and other issues, but also leads to additional chronic diseases and problems, etc... Make them interesting and make sure that you're allowed to give your business address and phone at the bottom of every article.

You'll be surprised how many new patients you get from that exposure. Oh yeah – make sure it's your doctor's name on the article – even if someone in your practice writes it as we want the doctor's name associated with it.

## Local Speaking Engagements:

As you'll soon figure out, Medicare patients are definitely the most lucrative patients for you to have, and I'll go into detail about why I believe that, later.

For now, though, I want you to consider finding out where your local AARP groups meet for their monthly luncheons, where the senior citizens meet for daily meals and get-togethers and contact the person in charge.

Tell them that you want your physician to come speak for 30 minutes on a monthly basis on different topics that affects the geriatric population, such as diabetes, hypertension, hyplipidemia, foot care, leg pain, arthritis, etc....
There are enough subjects that you could talk for 2 years and never cover the same subject twice. You'll find that not only will you pick up a lot of new Medicare patients, but many of their families will seek you out as their physician as well.

The nice thing about both of these genres is that they do not cost you any advertising dollars! The last avenue for getting new patients is a very professionally prepared website that not only describes the doctor, makes the doctor look like someone they want taking care of them with the doc's background, family information, where the doctor goes to church, etc... - but also tells about the staff. Who is the office manager and what are the manager's goals for the practice and the patients?

Tell about each staff member, with their photo (and make sure that every employee in the practice has their own business cards with the title of their position and you'll find those end up in hands of prospects that will lead them to your door). Talk about the services your clinic offers, the hours, what insurances are accepted, what do to in emergency, what your policies are for new patients, etc...

Also important on the website are the forms that you have for new patients. It's best to arrange it so the patient can complete these prior to arriving at your office.

You should also provide them a list of what they need to bring with them (drivers license, insurance card, prescription card, large denominations of cash, etc). You may be surprised at how many patients are checking out their local physicians BEFORE they pick their doctor, by surfing the web.

Give the patients a way (email address on the website) that they can email you questions while they are trying to decide if they want to come see you.

If you do not yet have a website where new patients can download these forms and practice information sheets, perhaps that would be a good place to start this week.

## Medicare Participation Status

Another decision that needs to be made, at least several months prior to seeing your first patient in your office will be your Medicare participation decision. To me – the answer is simple... ENROLL AS A PARTICIPATING PHYSICIAN, but let's examine what your 3 choices are and why I made that recommendation. The 3 choices you have are:

### Participating:

This means you will accept assignment on every covered Medicare covered service you provide. As a participating physician, you have a 5% higher Medicare allowed amount than you would have if you were non-participating. You're already required to file the claims and you're going to be subject to the same scrutiny and coding requirements, regardless if you're par or non-par. Being a par physician does NOT mean that you have to see every Medicare patient that calls for an appointment, but it does mean you'll accept Medicare's assignment on each one you do see.

### Non-Participating:

If you failed to sign the participation agreement, when you requested your Medicare number, then you are non-par and you have the choice whether to accept assignment or not accept assignment on a claim by claim basis. If you're non-par, you can accept the assignment on one patient and then not accept it on the next patient, if you wish. If you do accept assignment, your allowed amount will be 5% less than it would be if you were a participating physician. If you're going to see patients in the hospital or in the nursing home, where you'll probably accept assignment anyway, you'll make 5% less than if you were participating. Your fee to the Medicare patient can be collected at the time of service, from the patient, but your fee will be limited to the LIMITING CHARGE. That Limiting Charge is 15% above the non-par Medicare allowed amount, so you cannot charge and collect from the Medicare patient any amount you wish to. You are also still required to accept assignment on certain claims and specific services, such as clinical lab tests, regardless if you're par or non-par.

**Opted-Out:**

These are physicians that have sent a letter to the Secretary of the Health & Human Services (HHS) notifying them that for a period of not less than 2 years, they will opt-out of the Medicare program and any services they provide to Medicare patients (other than emergency services) will not be reimbursed by the Medicare program. I do not EVER recommend this option to any primary care physicians.

There are several reasons why I recommend all primary care physicians enroll in participating and they are mostly centered on the increased income that their clinics will enjoy by participating.

Not only do they get the 5% increased allowed amount, and the hospitals are required to refer patients to participating physicians, but 25 years of working with physicians have taught us that physicians will accept assignment routinely on specific patients, including:

1. Hospital patients (Physicians seem very reluctant to pick through the patient's purse or pants while

they are seeing hospital patients to get their money).

2. Skilled and Non Skilled Nursing Home patients: Ditto – the same thing

3. Office patients that receive expensive or extensive diagnostic testing in the clinic. The problem is also that the physicians that choose to not accept assignment are less likely to order or perform the diagnostic tests that the patients truly need, if they have to ask the patient for the money – thereby resulting in mediocre or inferior medical care being rendered to the patient.

4. Patients with Medicaid as secondary insurance (Patients with Medicaid as secondary usually – but not always – have very little money, so the opportunity to collect the Limiting Charge at the time of service is reduced).

## Medicare Pt Refuses Claims Filing

You may someday be presented with a Medicare patient that demands that you not file their claim to Medicare and they wish to pay for the service out of their own pocket. How do you handle it, since you do not wish to withdraw from the Medicare program entirely, yet you wish to honor the patient's request? The Medicare Carrier Manual addresses this. It says: "The only situation in which non-opt out physicians or practitioners, or other suppliers, are not required to submit claims to Medicare for covered services is where a beneficiary or his/her legal representative refuses, of his/her own free will, to authorize the submission of a bill to Medicare.

In this situation, the bill would not be submitted "on behalf of" the beneficiary. However, the limits on what the physician, practitioner or other supplier may collect from the beneficiary continue to apply to charges for the covered service, notwithstanding the absence of a claim to Medicare."

This means that you may not collect more than Medicare's allowable amount from the patient if you are participating or the Medicare Limiting Charge if you are not participating, even though you are not filing a claim to Medicare as the rules STILL protect the patient. You should also have the patient sign something refusing you permission to file the claim.

## Participation With Managed/Mangled Care Plans

(this is not a typo – as what some may consider managed care plans, I prefer to think of most of them as mangled care plans that get in the way of the patient-physician relationship)

It is also vital that you determine which, if any, of the managed care plans that you're going to participate or enroll with. In most practices, it is expected and usually considered good business, to enroll with those that will enable you to see the most patients, unless those plans result in you seeing more patients – but making less money.

Your local hospital will be able to tell you which plans carry the majority of patients in your area, and this is an area that you need to be careful about. Most plans carrying a lot of the patients will try to convince you to sign contracts for the lowest amount that you'll accept and in about 5 states (OH, PA, NY, NJ and MD and the central part of Florida), they have uncanny success at getting physicians to sign contracts for less than the Medicare allowed. We usually do not see that happening as much in places like Texas (where everyone has a license to carry a gun and those carriers are afraid of Texans).

In my opinion, signing the contracts at such a low amount is pitiful and if the physicians in these places would start saying no to the plans offering 86% of Medicare or 75% of Medicare, then those same carriers would be FORCED to start paying a decent rate. As long as most of the physicians are freely willing to whore themselves out to the carriers, they will be forcing other physicians in their area to under-value their services and accept these contracts.

In the meantime, you may want to consider the fact that Medicare patients may be the highest payer in your area, so you may want to concentrate your practice on those patients, see less patients, give BETTER care and make more money. We are not attorneys, but we do recommend you have your own attorney read any contract you're presented by a managed care company to sign, to protect yourself.

## Red Flag Laws

Per Federal law, you are required to make every reasonable attempt to verify the patient presenting to you is presenting their real name, address, and identifying information, short of obtaining fingerprints, retina scans, butt cheek scans and birth certificates. You're also required to protect that data, by the same laws. So, you need to determine what office policies you will have regarding the copying of drivers licenses on all new patients (we recommend you do copy them, or the passport or the military id – and it is legal to copy all three, by the way). It is probably a Good Idea for you to check out:
http://healthit.hhs.gov/portal/server.pt
which is the government's new website all about healthcare technology – and that also covers the Red Flag Laws.

## Provider Identity Theft

Several Medicare carriers are publishing the following letter on their website to members. This is serious and should be passed along to each of your employees, so that someone does not inadvertently or innocently give out information that could damage your practice and your providers.

"This is to inform you that Medicare is aware of an organized group who is representing themselves as either a Medicare Fraud Investigator; or a Medicare employee from the enrollment, claims or audit units.

These callers tell the physician, or office personnel, that the Medicare computer system has had a malfunction and they need to update lost information. The callers may also say they need to update the physician's provider record. They then request via telephone or fax the following information:

➢  Copy of Physician's Drivers License;

➢  Copy of Physician's Social Security Number (SSN);

➢  Unique Physician Identification Number (UPIN);

➢  Verification of education;

➢  Verification of Practice Location;

➢  Copy of Physician's Medical License;

➢  Copy of Patient's Charts for a specific period of time.

Once the entity receives this information, they falsify enrollment data (CMS 855 forms) using the physician's name and request a change to their practice locations, telephone numbers, and pay-to-addresses.

The Centers for Medicare & Medicaid Services (CMS) has not suffered any computer system malfunction and are not calling providers requesting the above information be provided. If you should receive such a call, please try to verify the telephone number of the caller, and immediately notify your Medicare carrier that you suspect fraud.

The CMS is committed to protecting all Medicare providers/suppliers and to ensuring that only those qualified make changes to enrollment data. We believe that with your help we can target those unscrupulous individuals that are looking to take advantage of you and the Medicare trust fund."

## Copying Patient's Driver License

Once again, the rumor mills are hard at work in spreading disinformation. The latest is that it is illegal to copy a driver's license in certain states. We have researched this and found NO states where it is illegal to make a black and white copy of a driver's license. Yes – there are some that swear this or that law exists – but as usual – when asked to present a copy, reference, legal cite, etc... - they come up empty.

What are some of the other FALSE **rumors** still circulating?

- You can't bill for multiple office visits in one day (you can, if they are not related)
- You can't bill for telephone calls to patients (non Medicare patients) (depends on payer)
- You can't swim for 30 minutes after eating
- You can't bill a no-show fee to Medicare patients (Medicare says you can)
- You can't collect the patient's co-pay prior to the patient seeing the doctor (wrong – do it)
- You can't send the patient a statement if they tell you not to (uh – yes you can)

- You can't call patients by name in the reception area (of course you can – but don't call them by illness, such as Mrs. Jones with the Hemorrhoids – come on back!)
- You can't use patient sign-in sheets – leaving the patients name on the sheet (HIPAA doesn't care, as long as you don't release clinical or financial info with it)
- You can't have the nurse document the ROS or PFSH. (not true – the nurse CAN document the chief complaint, ROS, PFSH and constitutional exam elements.)
- You can't collect the Medicare coinsurance until after the claim is processed  (false – collect it at the time of service!)
- You can't send a patient to collections until you've warned the patient  (no law requires you warn the patient, send them a telegram or a certified letter)
- You can't refuse to accept any new patients of any payment type (until Obama takes over COMPLETE care of your practice – you can!)

- You can't divorce patients for failure to follow office policy (You can divorce them for anything other than race, religion, sex, crerace, gender, religion, sexual orientation and disability. In fact, one doctor in Mt Dora Florida says he prefers to not see Obama voters!)

Remember to make anyone prove a law or regulation exists, if they say it does. It's impossible to prove something doesn't exist (usually), so put the burden on them to prove it does. If someone says you CAN'T do something – make them PROVE it!

## Copying Military Id Cards Is Legal

From the Tricare Provider Handbook - Copying ID Cards

Military personnel and their family members may express concern about having their military ID cards photocopied, perhaps because they have always been instructed never to lose or allow someone to use their card. These instructions are designed to prevent identity theft and safeguard against security being compromised by someone impersonating U.S. military personnel.

Although some TRICARE beneficiaries may believe that it's illegal to copy ID cards, it is in fact, legal to copy them for authorized purposes. The legitimate cardholder may allow his/her military or uniformed services ID card to be photocopied to facilitate medical care eligibility determination and documentation, check cashing, or the administration or other military-related benefits. Per TMA (Tricare Military Authority) instruction, it is both allowable and advisable for providers to copy the beneficiary's ID card for proof of eligibility and for the purpose of rendering needed services.

TMA recommends that providers copy both sides of the ID cards and retain copies for future reference.

Title, 18 USC, Section 701 prohibits photographing, or possessing uniformed services ID cards in an unauthorized manner. Unauthorized use would exist only if the bearer uses the card in a manner that would enable him/her to obtain benefits, privileges, or access to which he/she is not entitled.

## Patient Hesitant To Share SSN

If you have a patient that doesn't want to release their social security number to you, what will be your policy? If you expect to be able to turn them to a collection agency, you'll need it and their driver's license number.

Here is one way to explain to a patient why they need to release the social security number – if your practice requires the SSN. "I understand your hesitancy in giving me your SSN with all the news reports out there regarding identity theft. However, if you are wanting us to file this office visit to your insurance company, we will have to have your SSN because your insurance company has chosen that as your member ID number for us to file claims on your behalf. If you are having issues about giving me this number, then you will need to address this with your insurance carrier. But our contract with your insurance company states we will use the number they furnish us with for billing purposes only and that number is your SSN".

I reassure them this information is kept confidential and that we do not "sell" their number or use it in any way other that identity for billing.

I have also informed them that if they do not provide us with their SSN, then they could be in violation with their policy agreement and their insurance company may refuse to pay for the visit, making them fully responsible for this visit and all of the charges incurred. If the patient still does not want to release it to you and you are not comfortable making them pay in full for their services AT THE TIME OF SERVICE, we recommend you not accept that patient as a new patient. You're not obligated to see them, even if you are enrolled as a participating physician with Medicare or their carrier. In fact, you can turn away any patient that you do not wish to accept as a new patient in your practice, for payment purposes.

Are you going to have your staff email the packet (in PDF format) to the new patient when they call in for an appointment, so that they can have it completed prior to their arrival? Since the Star Trek transporter is not yet available, we should use the internet and email as often as we can. How often are you going to require your Medicaid patients present their Medicaid card, considering they can be enrolled or dropped from enrollment monthly on Medicaid? Generally, we recommend you make a copy of it every single time the patient comes to your office, so you can verify they still have coverage. Naturally, we also recommend you make a copy of the patient's insurance card (front and back) as that will have information that you will need for insurance filing. It's not a bad idea to ask patients to bring their policy with them on the first visit so you can copy the face-sheet that gives deductible, exclusion, when it is necessary to get a referral, etc...

## Copying Medicare Cards

Speaking of asking for insurance cards, let's discuss Medicare cards for a moment. Patients are constantly being approached by people selling Medicare Advantage (M.A.) plans and you may or may not be enrolled with the plan they choose.

The problem is that no matter how many times these salespeople explain to the patient that they are REPLACING their traditional Medicare plan, many will not realize that and believe they are buying a supplement or secondary plan or even a drug-plan. When your staff asks them if they have replaced their Medicare or whether they still have the same Medicare they had last month, they'll say yes – even though they do not. You will not realize they replaced traditional Medicare for an M.A. until you filed the claim to Medicare and received a denial and then you will not be successful at getting paid by the patient. For this reason, we suggestion your staff asks every Medicare patient if they have either replaced their Medicare or enrolled in a supplemental policy or enrolled in a drug-coverage plan since their last visit. When you say "drug-coverage" plan, many will reach into their wallet and hand you a card that shows they now have a Medicare Advantage plan instead of traditional Medicare.

# Prior To The Patient Arriving

I have never understood why most offices are not taking advantage of the tools available to them to make their jobs so much easier. For instance, 90% of medical offices wait until the patient arrives before handing them a clipboard with the new patient information form, history form, HIPAA Notice of Patient Privacy, Release of Information Form, Assignment of Benefits form, etc... They tell the patient to arrive 15 minutes early and less than half of the patients do, so when it is time for the nurse to be taking vitals and getting the chief complaint and preliminary review of systems on the patient, the patient is still completing the 147 pages of documents that they need to sign (OK – maybe not 147 pages – but it sure FEELS that way to the patients).

My advice is that when the patient calls in for a new patient appointment, that their email address be requested by the office personnel so that the forms can be emailed to the patient. If the patient doesn't want to give out the email or the staff doesn't want to mess with that (ok – if they don't want to "mess with that" – get rid of the staff and get staff that are willing to do their job – but that is a different subject), then at least have the forms all downloadable on the clinic's website. Yes, in spite of what you may be thinking, the majority of patients have internet access and emails (even some of the 87 year old ones do!).

But, if you do not ASK for their email address – you won't get it. It's funny how life works that way. The Bible even covers that in John 16:24 where Jesus said "ask, and ye shall receive". I believe that most offices are not getting the information they need (or the co-pays and co-insurances) because they simply DO NOT ASK.

Not everyone is comfortable asking, and many medical clinics have the WRONG person sitting at the front desk.  They have timid Suzie there that is afraid, embarrassed, scared, and uncomfortable asking for money.  Interestingly, Suzie's last job was a cashier at the local grocery store and she had no problem asking for the $68.12 when the people were buying food, sodas, cigarettes and produce, but she doesn't like asking for money at the desk.  PUT SUZIE IN A DIFFERENT JOB!!!!

Ok – so we ask for the patient to complete the information at home so that it is complete when they get to the office, but do we also give them a list of what we want them to bring to the office with them?

- Drivers' License or Photo Identification:  (we do get this on every new patient, and if we do not do so – then our elevators stop short of the top floor! )
- Insurance Card
- List of Medications We're taking (or the actual bottles containing the pills so that your staff can see which ones need refilling – which is much better in my opinion)

## When The Patient Arrives

What kind of reception does the patient receive when they walk into your office? What does the new patient see and experience when they enter your office for the first time?

- Is the office clean?  Is it professionally cleaned or is it obvious that the staff just straightened it?

- Are there so many pieces of paper on the walls that they can't see what color the wallpaper is? Does the office look professional?
- Are there magazines everywhere? How old are the magazines and in what condition? Are the magazines the kind that your patients would be interested in? Is the print on the magazines large enough for all patients to read?
- What condition is the furniture in? Would you be afraid to sit on the furniture, knowing that the person who sat on it before you may have had all kinds of illnesses? Is it comfortable or does it appear too cheap?
- Is there a television playing in the reception area? Is it too loud or too soft? Is it playing information about your practice or is it playing Disney movies or soap operas? You may want to use one of the services that can be programmed to inform the patients about the services your office offers, the hours, etc...
- Is there some kind of board stating that your physician is running 15 minutes late? Does it ALWAYS state that your physician is 30 minutes late?
- Are there enough chairs for everyone to have a seat?
- Are there toys for small children laying around to be tripped over? Does the reception area offer the patients the chance to hear every conversation the receptionist or office personnel have? Is there some kind of glass or separation?
- Is there some kind of "overhead" music to help block out confidential information being discussed? Is it too loud or too soft?

- Is there a sign-in sheet that each person should sign as they arrive? What does it ask? Is the print large enough for the elderly to read? Contrary to what many believe, it is not illegal per HIPAA (Health Insurance Portability and Accountability Act) to have a patient sign-in sheet, and this will be discussed in the HIPAA section. . If you share a reception area with others, is it clear to the new patient where to check in? It's amazing how many times I've been to an office to see a new client and stood in the reception area trying to figure out where to check in.
- Is there enough light for the patients to read by? Is it too bright so that your patients want to put their sunglasses back on?

Once the patient arrives and has completed their new patient form, history form, and presented their identification, are you giving them something that explains YOUR office policies so they know the rules and what is expected?

- Does the new patient know that co-pays will be collected prior to seeing the doctor or that co-insurance will be collected prior to their leaving?
- Do you accept credit cards and if so – which ones? By the way – if you're not accepting credit cards – join the 21st century and start accepting at least MasterCard, Visa and Discover as it makes more sense to collect it now and pay the 2% fee than to have to send statements to the patients and hope they pay you. I personally do not accept American Express in my own

business, as they seem to cost me more than MasterCard, Visa and Discover.

# Prescription Refills

What is your policy on prescription refills? Have you adopted the policy (that we recommend) of not refilling prescriptions over the phone and/or fax or do you get 30 phone calls and faxes each day that requires a person half a day handling it? If you require all patients to bring with them, to every visit, every drug they are taking, you can avoid the phone calls.

Once the patient arrives with their Wal-Mart bag or plastic baggie with their prescriptions, you can have your M.A., nurse or whomever gets the vitals, to go through them and make sure they are on the list you prescribed and see which ones are going to run out before the next visit and you can refill them during the visit. This counts towards the medical decision making portion of the visit. If the patient doesn't bring their drugs with them to the visit, and they do call in for a refill, they can be told "We no longer refill over the phone, as you noticed on the patient information sheet we had you sign, so you need to schedule an appointment with Stephanie (your nurse or M.A.) to review your medications and we'll refill your prescriptions on that visit". This way, instead of Stephanie being an expense in your practice, spending half a day each day faxing, calling, pulling charts and ambushing you in the hallway between patients to get your ok on another refill, she is generating 99211s for you. Medicare's allowed in 2009 was about $17, so if she just does this 3 times a day, you're looking at another $13,000 a year in income instead of costing you money.

It also will knock out 25 phone calls a day – while helping you practice better medicine.

The reason it helps you clinically is because you will soon find out which of your patients are getting drugs from other physicians or the Veterans Administration that you are not aware of, and some of those may be contra-indicated with the meds you are prescribing.

## No-Show Fee

Do you have a no-show policy that results in the patient having to pay a fee? If not – then you are not holding your patients responsible for keeping their appointments and there is no negative consequence to them not keeping their appointment. When they fail to keep their appointment, they are showing disrespect to you and your valuable time. I recommend you consider charging the non-Medicaid patient a fee of $25 for missing an office visit and a $50 fee for no-showing on a scheduled procedure. If there is no negative consequence to a negative action, then people will continue to perform the negative action. That is the same reason why there is a fine for speeding, illegal parking, etc...

As a parent, did you not institute some kind of penalty for failing to follow rules, such as a spanking or grounding if your child skipped school? If you didn't have the penalty, then there was nothing to make the child follow the rules and the same thing applies to your patients.

Yes – I know that many have a 3 strike rule saying that if you miss 3 appointments, then you'll be discharged from the practice.

This is the same thing as telling your child that they do not have to obey you the first 2 times that you tell them something (I'll count to 3!!!!).    I have NEVER, in 26 years, had a client tell me that they lost even one patient that they didn't want to lose, because they instituted a policy of charging for no-shows.  You cannot charge a no-show fee to Medicaid (per CMS), but you can charge it to everyone else – including Medicare patients (but not the Medicare program) – so go for it.  In fact, in some states, if the state makes the appointment for the patient (such as workers comp), you'll find the state will pay the fee. As to Medicaid, you SHOULD notify Medicaid in your state every time a Medicaid patient doesn't keep their appointment as well and inform your Medicaid patients that failure to keep those appointments COULD result in them losing their Medicaid privileges.

Another option with Medicaid patients is to take away their appointment privilege and explain "Since you failed to keep your appointment, you have lost the privilege of scheduling appointment for six months.  For the next six months, if you wish to see the doctor, you'll need to be "worked in", which may require a wait.   At the end of six months, your privilege to schedule an appointment will be restored"

You can also divorce your Medicaid patient for failing to keep their appointments, but make sure that policy is in what you give the patients on their first visit.  By the way – a no-show fee is NOT charging an office visit code – as that would be fraudulent billing.  You can create your own 5 digit code (since most computer programs are designed to hold CPT and HCPCS codes – which are 5 digits), such as NOSHO or MISSD or something similar. Each month, when you run your reports, you'll be able to see how many no-shows you had.    Also – the question comes up about whether you should hold the patient responsible to pay for the no-show fee if you ever have to turn the account to collection.    The answer is YES!!! They owe it.    Does your bank hold you responsible for paying the over-draft fee when YOU bounce a check? Does your Mortgage Company or utility hold you responsible for paying a late payment fee?

Of course they do – because they treat you like an adult – and it is definitely time you did the same with your patients.

## The Reception Area

Too often, the reception area does not reflect the kind of professionalism the physician or manager wishes to portray. Try stepping out of your office and then walking into the reception area and look around. What do you see? What do you hear?  Are your patients greeted in a friendly way when they walk in?   Are they treated the way YOU would want to be treated?  Have a seat and listen for a few minutes and notice what your patients hear while sitting in your reception area.  What do you smell? Is it inviting to you or does it make you uncomfortable. If it bothers you  –  remember that it bothers your patients too. This is the first visual "first-impression" that many of your patients have with your practice. You only get one chance to make a first-impression – so make sure it is the impression that you wish to make.

I've been in some reception areas (get away from calling it a 'waiting room" as that has a definite negative connotation in the minds of patients) that were not clean or comfortable. I was in one that had cloth chairs and cloth couches. EXCUSE ME! The person sitting there before me had WHAT disease? I don't think that I want to sit there. I remember one office that had a television going that definitely needed repair and only half of the screen was working. I returned to that office about 3 weeks later and it was the SAME WAY. What does this tell your patients?

Uh – it tells me that someone who is not paying attention to the details in their reception area probably doesn't pay that much attention to details such as cleanliness, sanitary equipment, accuracy on records, etc... and I'm probably not alone in that view.

In another office, the television was set to a Spanish speaking station only, and I asked all 5 people in the reception area if any of them spoke Spanish. None did – yet the receptionist spoke Spanish and guess who was watching the soap opera from her desk.... Very unprofessional!

## Why Patients Leave Clinics

I remember a report I read back in the early 90s about why a patient will leave one practice and go to another. I don't remember all of the reasons, but I do remember the first 7:

1.  The physician has an "I don't care" attitude or talks over my head and doesn't take the time to help me understand my own treatment or condition.
2.  The staff treats me like they're doing me a favor by taking care of me.
3.  Which managed care plans or insurance does the practice accept
4.  How close to my home or work is this practice
5.  How clean and comfortable is the reception area – including how current the magazines are
6.  What hours the practice is open
7.  What are the fees they charge

Think about this. The cleanliness of the reception area is MORE important to patients than the FEES you charge.

I've been in an OB/GYN office that had sporting and hunting magazines in the reception area and no magazines designed for women's interests. Yes – I know that some women like sports (I'm blessed that my wife likes NFL as much as I do – if not more) and some like to hunt – but by and large – most women prefer other type of magazines. They also need to be in good taste as well. You do not want the February edition of Sports Illustrated sitting in your reception area if you see a lot of geriatric men or you may be needing the defibrillator and calling 911, as February is the Swimsuit edition. Make sure your magazines are appropriate to your type of patients and their interests.

Also – you need to police the type of television shows you have on the television if you have a television in your reception area as some are DEFINITELY not suitable for a professional image. I really do not care what your receptionist watches at home – but you should care what she puts on the television in your reception area.

## Collecting The Deductible And/Or Co-Insurance

Almost every insurance plan in the country has a deductible the patient needs to meet, prior to the benefits of the plan paying reimbursement. For instance, we have a private policy that has a $10,000 deductible that must be met prior to the carrier paying anything.

Medicare Part B has a $155 deductible (in 2010) that applies to E&M, procedures and diagnostic tests.

Their deductible does not apply to the following:

- Screening mammography.
- Clinical diagnostic laboratory tests (including specimen collection fees) performed or supervised by a physician, laboratory, or other entity paid on an assigned basis;
- Pneumococcal vaccine and its administration;
- Influenza vaccine and its administration; and
- Services or items denied as medically unnecessary.
- Welcome to Medicare (IPPE) physical

So, when the Medicare patient is about to leave your office, after seeing the doctor, the receptionist should:

1. Determine whether the patient has met their deductible or not (if it's within the first few days of the year, it's probable that the patient has not met their deductible for the new year) and note the amount of the deductible (In 2010, it is $155 for Medicare Part B services)

2. Review the Medicare allowed for the office visit and any procedures performed and if the deductible has NOT been met, apply those amounts towards the deductible.

As an example, if the Office visit has a Medicare allowed of $53.50 and the removal of impacted cerumen has an allowed of $24.50, you would total the 2 allowed to $78.00 and since that is below the $155 deductible, you'd ask the patient to pay the $78.00 today. Yes – in spite of what you may have heard at the Laundromat or the latest office manager meeting, you ARE allowed to collect the deductible at the time of service, if you know the patient has not met it.

When you file the claim, the first $155 will apply to the deductible, and there is no reason why you should have to go to the trouble of preparing a statement, folding it, placing it in the envelope and then having to spend postage to send the statement to collect what you can and should collect today while the patient is in front of you. It is much easier to collect the deductible and co-insurance in the office than it is through the mail or while the patient is in the hospital ("yes, doctor, I want you to go through the patient's purse while she is in a coma on your hospital rounds and collect $155 from her and leave this receipt in her wallet" may not be acceptable practice yet).

Along these same lines, if the patient HAS met their deductible, then you should collect 20% of the Medicare allowed on the visit and procedures and diagnostics while the patient is present – unless the patient has a co-insurance, supplemental insurance or Medigap plan, in which case the deductible and/or co-insurance may be paid by them after Medicare automatically forwards the EOB to them.

If your insurance carrier or the patient tells you that you are not allowed to collect the co-pay, co-insurance or deductible at the time of service, make them PROVE their statement with something in writing that is official. I have NEVER seen a policy that prohibited it – in spite of hearing that they exist. In every instance when I asked to see the contract language that prohibited it, no one has ever been able to present it to me.

## Fees & Discounts

You can buy several dozen books on setting fees for a medical practice and buy the computer programs that allows you to plug in the relative value units times the local geographical practice cost indices and a variety of conversion factors to come up with a fee – but why?

If you're really into Relative Value Units and knowing WHY you should charge specific charges, then we highly recommend you check out http://www.mitsi.org/html/home.html, which is the website for MIT Solutions and Frank Cohen. Frank is an expert at statistics, data analysis, trends, analytic processes, RBRVS and RVU analysis, and more. He has webinars on these subjects and is definitely respected in the medical community.

As to calculating the Medicare allowed amounts, Medicare has already done that work for you. You can download the Medicare numbers at CMS' website or even at www.donself.com for free. You can see what Medicare's allowed amounts are if the service is performed in your office or in the hospital (many codes have a lower allowed in the hospital as the physician has lower overhead and expense when performing the procedure there instead of their office) and all of that information doesn't cost you a cent.

## Setting the fees

If you're been reading my newsletter or articles for long, you know that I normally recommend you have one fee schedule set at about two times the Medicare allowed amount, although in 49 states—there is no restriction on you having multiple fee schedules. Texas is different. It is the only state that I know of that has mandated— through insurance code—that you charge all **insurance plans** the same fee. Section 552 of the Texas Insurance code does exclude:

(1) Medicaid or Medicare patient or a patient who is covered by a federal, state, or local government-sponsored indigent health care program;

(2) financially or medically indigent person who qualifies for indigent health care services based on:
    (A) a sliding fee scale; or
    (B) a written charity care policy established by a health care provider; or

(3) person who is not covered by a health insurance policy or other health benefit plan

The Texas insurance code says a person commits an offense, which is a Class B misdemeanor, if:

(1) the person knowingly or intentionally charges two different prices for providing the same product or service; and
    (2) the higher price charged is based on the fact that an insurer will pay all or part of the price of the product or service.

So—if you are anywhere other than Texas—you can have multiple fee schedules (to the best of my knowledge), but if you're in Texas, you should charge each of your private insurance plans the same fee. You can have a charity policy whereby you give a person with no insurance any break you wish to since the section does not apply to patients without insurance.

Many office managers advise their physicians to charge two to three times Medicare's allowed amounts and that seems to be a pretty safe way to set your fees. Consider the fact that it doesn't matter what you charge a Medicare patient on an assigned claim, since Medicare's allowed amount will determine how much you can actually collect. The fact that most of the private carriers and managed care plans have a set amount they will pay (many are also based on Medicare's rate) or they may even negotiate with you at a percentage of Medicare also reinforces the thought that it doesn't matter what you charge – as long as you're charging above the amount they will allow you to collect. The problem arises when I see physicians or managers that set their fees at what they THINK Medicare's allowed will be or at the amount they THINK the private/managed plan will approve. That is almost always a mistake and the reasoning behind it is (in my opinion) flawed. Some physicians believe that if they charge what Medicare allows, then their adjustments will be less and somehow – that makes the earth spin on its axis better or that it saves them money.

Some managers promote this idea as it makes their collection percentages appear higher. Both reasons are flawed, if you truly realize what collection ratios and adjustments are.

# Adjustments:

There are 3 basic kinds of adjustments to patient balances in medical accounting:

**Contractual Adjustments**: These are the adjustments or write-offs that reflect the difference between the amount allowed to be collected on a particular contract and the amount charged. As an example, let's assume you're charging $100 for 99213 and Medicare's allowed is $59.50. That means that you'll have a $40.50 contractual adjustment. That's normal and does not reflect negatively on the billing agency, manager or staff. If Blue Cross has an approved amount of $80.00, and you charged $100, then you have a $20 contractual adjustment.

**Bad Debt Adjustment**: This is the amount written off because you can't collect it, for whatever reason. This is the amount that reflects negatively on the billing agency, staff and managers. When you turn an account to a collection agency, the amount should be adjusted off to bad debt and should not be carried on the normal accounts receivable.

**Courtesy or Professional Adjustments**: These are the adjustments that we make by choice because we want to give another physician a break, a discount to the employee, a discount to the clergy, military, etc...

These should be monitored – but again – do not reflect negatively on the billing agency, staff or managers.

The accounts receivable should be kept clean for several reasons, including for bankers as collateral for a loan if you ever need it. Bankers will not loan money on a sloppy accounts receivable, but many will loan up to 70% on a clean and truthful A/R.

Another reason for a clean A/R is that the A/R is an asset of the business and if the business owner (such as physician) passes away – you do not want the spouse paying estate taxes on uncollectable money, so keep the A/R clean.

## Self-Pay Agreement

While I have NEVER seen an instance where an overzealous government attorney or prosecutor has chosen to attack a physician on the Stark Self-Referral or "Incentive-to-refer" implications in the laws, I have been repeatedly told that these exist. OK – so does this mean that you can't give a self-pay patient a break? Not in my opinion, but I am not an attorney and I do not play one on television. I have spent multiple nights at Holiday Inn Express, so that means that I have some inherent knowledge (if we are to believe the commercials on television). OK – here is something that should protect you in case you decide to give a cash patient a break on their bill. Have the patient sign this form:

> I,
>
> _____
>
> ____, ("Patient/Guarantor") wish to negotiate a payment arrangement for services rendered on the date of service referenced above. Furthermore, I declare that I do not have health insurance of any kind and this payment negotiation is not based on any possible referrals that could be made by me.

Once you have the patient sign the above form, you should be covered.

Once again, we recommend you give patients a break when they need it – but just because someone has no insurance, that doesn't mean they can't afford it – as they may choose to spend the money on other elective things instead of insurance.  How many patients have you seen that are driving nicer cars than you office manager, carrying purses that cost more than the High School Class Ring that you bought your high school senior and carrying an expensive IPOD or IPhone and they ask you for a break because they have no insurance.

They may be choosing to pay for 220 cable channels, a Wii, name brand jeans and choosing NOT to pay for health insurance.

## Double Booking – Double Trouble

I was on the phone awhile back with a practice that is wondering why their numbers have declined from seeing 31 patients a day to 24.  I asked the manager if they double book and the answer was "we have to, due to the number of no-shows".  This is just like saying "I started cleaning my son's room for him since the bum refuses to do it himself, and I don't have the guts to be a good parent".

DUH!!!  Ok – the answer is to hold your patients responsible by charging for a no-show.  If you reduce the no-shows, then you won't have to disrespect your patients by double booking.
A recent report published by the AMA says that physicians should consider over-booking appointments if they have a very high no-show rate to help compensate for the lost income.   They even compared this to the

over-booking policy at airlines. Before you jump on this idea, let's consider a few things.

If a plane overbooks, then 1 or 2 people get bumped off and the rest of the passenger takes off on the flight and gets to their destination either on time or close to it. If you over-book in your office, and your number of no-shows is lower than usual that day, then EVERYONE will end up being delayed and your staff will start seeing patients grumbling about waiting an hour or two. You may even see a patient or two walk out after deciding that it's not worth it to wait. That's a big difference.

If an airline overbooks, then it may or may not even affect the amount of customers they have. Take for instance, Tyler Texas. There are only 2 airlines fly into or out of there and one goes to Houston and one goes to DFW airport. Neither has any competition.

If folks get bumped, they grumble about it, but the next time they have to fly – they're still using one of these 2 airlines instead of driving hours each way to get to another one. It's not that way in your office.

If you make the patients wait too long, then it isn't long before they are looking at doctors that are 5 minutes away – not hours.

Instead of giving drugs to cover up the symptoms (which is what over-booking does), why not address the problem – which is the number of no-shows you have. Is there a negative consequence on the FIRST no-show? Do your patients know your policy regarding no-shows?

If you actually require credit card info and you bill their credit card for EVERY no-show, you'll find the number of no-shows diminishing. That's a fact. I do not recommend over-booking or double booking. That shows disrespect for your patients in my opinion.

## Divorce Poem To Patient

You can and should divorce patients for failure to follow your office policies, failure to pay their bills or if they are rude to your staff. You're welcome to use the following:

I've written this note to inform you,
That your privileges have been rescinded.
You've been discourteous and rude,
And my staff has been offended!

Now, you're welcome to find another
To care for your medical needs,
The County Medical Society,
Can provide you with some leads.

We will continue to see you,
For thirty days and no more
But only for an emergency,
Shall you cross and enter our door.

We will forward your records as requested
To the doctor of your choice
But warn others of your debts and actions,
We shall not do by letter or voice

So this letter is our notice to you
Sent by certified mail at a pittance
In parting, we wish to express..
Goodbye, Farewell, Good Riddance

# 47 Million Uninsured?

Many politicians embraced the numbers published by the Centers for Disease Control in June 2009, when they reported an estimated 43.8 million Americans had no health insurance in 2008, That is 700,000 more people than in 2007 and 2.8 million more than in 1997. Massachusetts had the lowest percentage of uninsured residents under age 65 (3.4%), and Texas had the highest (22.9%). An estimated 8.9% of children had no health insurance, the same as in 2007 but down from 13.9% in 1997.   This gave the White House and both chambers of Congress the ammunition they needed to convince people that we have a healthcare crisis in this country.... The New York Times came out with an interesting article on August 23, 2009.

In this  article, at  the NY Times (one of the most liberal papers in the country), they pointed out that it appears (if these numbers are correct) that about 45.7 million people are uninsured in this country, and of that 45.7 million:

- 9 Million live in a household making at least $75,000 a year - yet they choose to not get insurance - but I wonder how many in that household have cable or satellite channels, cell phones, IPods, personal computers, cigarettes, beer, and they choose to not buy insurance, but how many of them buy lottery tickets.

- 6 Million live in a household making at least $88,000 a year and..... they choose to not spend their money on insurance.

- About 5% of the 13 Million young adult folks who choose to not get insurance because they are young and healthy probably make more than $60,000 a year - but they'd rather spend their money on other things.

- About 9 million are not US Citizens and maybe 6 million of them are illegal aliens that will not be helped by Obamacare anyway.

- Approximately 11 million of them qualify for Medicaid - but because either they because they do not know they are eligible or are intimidated by the application process. So - perhaps if Obama was to spend some of that money to educate these people to what is available to them today instead of using it for Obamacare, we may not need a NEW public option. We have a public option now that is not being utilized by 11 million?

This is more than 34 of the 45.7 million that either do not truly NEED a new public option or they are not taking advantage of what they can have now.

(Uh – did I warn you at the beginning of the book that I may be considered politically incorrect?)

## Collecting The Co-Pay Prior To Seeing The Doctor

It amazes me how many offices were reticent or hesitant in collecting the managed care insurance co-pay prior to taking the patient back to the physician for their visit.

If the patient isn't going to pay, then the time to know that is BEFORE the services are rendered.

You do not see McDonalds, Burger King, Wendy's, Taco Bell, Dairy Queen or Church's Chicken giving you your food BEFORE you pay – and amazingly – they never have an accounts receivable problem with their customers. What do you think the manager of Arbys would say if you told them to please give you the Beefy Cheese and to send you a bill?

If the patient doesn't have their co-pay, and you know it before the patient receives treatment or services, then it's really easy for the receptionist to say "Mr. Jones, the doctor is running a little late and there is an ATM down the street at the convenience store". (As she pulls out $1.00), she says "while you're there getting your co-pay, can you please pick me up a Dr. Pepper?" She says it with a smile and the patient will either magically come up with the co-pay ("Oh – I forgot that I had this $50.00 bill in my other pocket"). You are NOT violating any laws by asking the patient to go get their co-pay.

The hospital has laws requiring them to triage the patient before ever mentioning money or some other stupid law – but that doesn't apply to privately owned physician offices. Until some liberal president nationalizes healthcare and makes all private healthcare companies subject to additional ridiculous laws, it's still private enterprise, so go for it and collect that co-pay at the time of service.

Now – if the patient has a head wound is bleeding all over the place or they stop breathing or something else that is obviously critical – you will be taking care of that patient before you ask for money.

To the receptionists: I want you going after that money at the window with the same intensity that you would if it were your OWN money that you would use to pay your own bills, buy your own food, pay for your own kid's orthodontics, etc.... if you are not giving it that much diligence, then you are not treating your employer the way you should and that extends to you office managers as well.

The following was a thread of a conversation on a Family Practice listserv that I monitor:

Q. If a patient doesn't pay their bill (and that bill was generated because they had not met their deductible per their insurance Company's EOB) after such time that we have written it off as bad debt, is there any way to notify their insurance Company that they never paid that share of their deductible so they are not credited by their carrier as having paid that portion of their deductible?

Interestingly, several people replied and stated that they send a notification to the Patient's insurance when the patient doesn't pay the deductible or co-insurance and in some cases the carriers have actually notified the patient that they were in danger of having their policy cancelled. The number of carriers that have threatened the patients was small, but you never know if the account that you.ve having to eat has a carrier that actually gives a darn.

Whether the carrier cares or not, the letter you send to the carrier (and COPY to the patient) may prompt the patient to get their posterior into your office and pay that delinquent amount. What do YOU have to lose (other than the 43 cents postage) by sending a letter to the carrier and copying the patient. I may even suggest you word it similarly to:

*Dear Insurance Adjudicator:*
*The above referenced claim required the patient to pay their deductible and/or coinsurance of $____, per the terms of your contract with the policyholder. After repeatedly sending statements to your policyholder, they have failed to pay that amount on the referenced claim. It is our understanding that failure to pay the co-insurance and/or deductible can result in the cancellation of the policy, per the terms of the policy.*

*Please feel free to contact us should you wish to confirm the non payment by your policyholder.*
Again . what do you have to lose? Imagine the satisfaction it will give you when the patient comes into your office with a check to rectify the situation.

## Office And Insurance Theft/Fraud

I'm telling the front office staff to treat it like it's your own money – UNTIL you collect it – but stop there – because if you treat it like it's your own after you collect it, we're talking embezzlement and that is not only illegal – it's WRONG and you will be caught and if your physician asks me, I'll recommend they prosecute and have you arrested.

I did when my own office manager embezzled from me around 1990 and I recommend it to my clients as well. If you do not prosecute, then you may be enabling them to go down the street and do the same thing to another physician.

In the middle 80's, I remember an office manager in Arlington, Texas that had been always been rude to me when I called on them to sell them super bills (those are the forms that physicians used to give patients as a receipt – that allowed the patient to file their own insurance claims). For months, she would never let me talk to the doctor and was adamant about him not discussing our accounts receivable programs.

One day, while making my normal monthly calls on the clinic, I noticed a very harried woman at the reception window and disarray at her desk. There were ledger cards and day sheets everywhere and I asked if Doris (not real name) was there and she said "hell no" and I knew then that there was a problem. I asked if Doris had been fired and was there some kind of accounts receivable problem and the woman explained that she was the doctor's wife and they believed that embezzlement had taken place. I spent a couple of days helping them reconstruct their ledgers and day sheets and to the best of our ability, we identified more than $65,000 had been taken (not very creatively either). I recommended the doctor prosecute – but he listened to others who convinced him not to.

Several months later, I found Doris in an office in Bedford working for another doctor and there was no way I was going to get to talk to the doctor.

I did leave a business card on the doctor's car (he had a sign over his space in the carport behind his office) saying that he may want to call the doctor in Arlington that Doris had previously worked for and gave him the phone number of the Arlington doctor. I understood that she left there – after embezzling and went to work for a doctor in Fort Worth. None of the doctors prosecuted and that just helped her get away with doing it to others.

When I see someone as adamant about not letting me talk to the doctor, it makes me wonder if the office manager is doing a really GOOD job of taking care of the doctor or if they are just TAKING CARE of themselves. I read once that the AMA said that 1 out of every 3 office suffer embezzlement or theft. After working in this business for 26 years, I'm of the belief that it's probably 1 in every 2. Embezzlement is the fraudulent appropriation of money or other assets by someone entrusted with it's care on behalf of others, but who uses it for his/her own purposes. If your employee takes paper clips home to their kids to use on a school project – that is considered employee theft.

It is sad to think of the number of people that would condemn shoplifting if they were to see it, but they think nothing of taking home a stapler, highlighter, ream of copier paper, bandaids, ace-wrap, etc... and justify it because "they don't pay me enough". One of the most common types of theft that I've seen are the employees who make long distance calls to friends or relatives – on the company phone. Or, they are stealing TIME by working on their resume or Facebook page or helping their children with their homework – WHILE THEY ARE BEING PAID TO WORK.

If you were paying an employee to clean your home, would you be upset to see them watching television instead of cleaning – during the hours you're paying them?

Theft is theft – regardless of its value or form and if you do it or if you know it is happening and you are not reporting it – you're guilty of it.   If someone came into your home and was stealing silverware, dishes, toothpaste, etc... that you bought – you would consider it dishonest – and we need to have the same principle in our office.

Along the same lines, when we are discussing theft, we need to discuss when medical offices are stealing from patients or insurance carriers.   Remember – when someone steals from an insurance carrier – they are stealing from every policyholder of that insurance company as the company will make up for it through increased premiums.   Insurance theft should be considered no less personal than you reaching into your patient's wallet and taking money that you are not entitled to and if you know of someone committing insurance fraud, the right thing is to make them stop. Sometimes it happens through mistakes or incorrect judgments and sometimes it is intentional.

If you discover that you are billing for something that is not being provided, should you immediately stop and then notify the carrier that you have been improperly paid?
That sounds like the honest thing to do.  Compare that to you giving a grocery store clerk a $10 bill for a $3 purchase and she gives you $17 back, thinking you had given her a $20.  If your son, daughter or grandchild was

sitting there watching this – what lesson would you teach them?

More importantly, even if they were not with you – what would YOU do?   If you're the type of person that would keep the money, thinking "it was their mistake, so I get to benefit from it", please put this book down now, contact me and send me the book and I'll buy it back for the price you paid as I do not want you benefiting from this book.   On the other hand, if you're the type that would give the money back to the clerk, then you should do the same thing with the money from the insurance carrier that was truly overpaid to you.  This applies, in my opinion, on instances where the insurance carrier double-paid on a claim.  In that case, there can be no question that you were over-paid.

It gets a little more tricky when the carrier paid you properly and a year or two later, they contact you and tell you that one code should have been bundled into another.

They may be using a new edit that was not in effect then or even an internal edit that no other carrier uses – but you get the demand from them for repayment.  Now, it is too late for you to effectively collect from the patient, so do you really owe them the money?   You rendered the service and on behalf of the patient, you accepted assignment.   If instead of sending the check directly to you, if they had sent the check to the patient and the patient presented that check to you, would YOU owe the insurance carrier the money or would the patient?  Who received the services?

You were paid on BEHALF OF the patient, so if any repayment to the insurance carrier is due, shouldn't it be due from the patient? After all – it was the patient that received the services.

Along these same lines, though, if you knew at the time of service that the carrier should not have been paying for that service, then the honest thing to do – back then – was to notify the carrier that an overpayment had occurred, so time does not diminish your culpability and responsibility to make sure the right thing is done.

Insurance fraud is rampant in this country and you can barely go a month without seeing a headline indicating someone is indicted or jailed for insurance fraud.

More than 10 years ago, I was working with a company in south Florida that provided a diagnostic piece of equipment to physicians and the physicians would bill the patient and/or insurance for the professional component and this company would bill Medicare and the other carriers for the technical component. If done correctly, this was perfectly legal and acceptable by all of the insurance carriers. I discovered that the company had been billing incorrectly to Medicare and the other payers for their services and as a result, they received about 20 times the amount they should have been paid. I had a meeting in an airport with the CEO of that company and explained that a mistake must have been made by their billing people and he told me "there is no mistake and this is how we should be paid, as the other way doesn't pay us enough".

I argued with him, unsuccessfully that it was insurance fraud and that if they continued, I had no choice but to notify the federal officials as well as pull every one of my clients away from their service and recommend a different service that would do it legally and ethically. He didn't believe me, so I did.    I worked with the OIG and Medicare and they were subsequently put out of business.

On three different occasions, in my consulting, I've discovered physicians that were billing improperly to increase their income and on all 3 occasions, I warned them that they were committing fraud and all 3 continued their practices.   I turned all 3 clinics into Medicare and the O.I.Gg, and I did not file a Qui Tam (Whistleblower suit) in order to receive a reward from the government.   I turned them in because it was the right thing to do and all 3 practices were suspended from the Medicare program and fined.   I'll continue to do so, which should be a warning to those reading this book and considering hiring me.   If you desire to defraud insurance, the government, the patients or anyone else – don't call me.  If you're doing it accidentally, I'll help you to rectify it and keep you compliant so to keep you out of trouble.  You can make a very good living in a medical practice without resorting to thievery or dishonesty.

If you lose your job because you have tried to get your employer to stop committing fraud or abuse, and they would not cease, then Qui Tam may be a way for you to recover what you've lost by becoming unemployed.   In common law, a writ of qui tam is a writ whereby a private individual who assists a prosecution can receive all or part of any penalty imposed.

The government has a program centered around Qui Tam (also called the Whistleblower Act) that allows you to receive up to 20% of the fine that is assessed against an entity that is found guilty of fraud against the federal government. I believe some states also have similar programs for state government fraud as well. The 1986 amendment to the False Claims Act (this is the act that embodies the Qui Tam) increased the minimum that the relator (person bringing the suit on behalf of the government) is awarded to 15%, with the maximum being 30%.

I believe the difference between the 2 is determined by whether the relator uses their own attorney or whether the relator uses the federal government attorneys. If you intend to file an action, you may want to talk to your own attorney before talking to the federal officials – as you may be giving 5% to 15% away by talking to the feds first. Also – in 1986, the amount of fines that can be assessed by the federal government increased to "treble damages", meaning that if someone stole $1 Million dollars in fraudulent claims, then the fine could be $3 Million against that party. There are attorneys in almost every major city in the U.S. that specialize in Qui Tam cases, but hopefully, if you know of someone defrauding the government, you'll be able to convince them to cease without having to turn them in to the feds. Again – if you lose your job by doing what is right – then you should seriously consider this option.

## The Medical Office Manager

Think of the Navigator on a ship. The Captain can make the decisions as to what will happen on that ship, but it is the navigator that ensures the ship gets to the right port. That is the medical office manager. Of course, the manager is also the chief boatswain, engineer, steward, deck hand, pilot, harbor pilot, docking pilot, fireman, cook, machinist, yeoman, mate, first ship's officer, second ship's officer, entertainment officer, grievances officer, carpenter, electrician, crows nest mate, as well as his or her own job of making sure that everyone does their job too. This position is the one that SHOULD make the day to day decisions, management decisions, hiring and firing decisions, be an expert at accounts receivable, accounts payable, scheduling, inventory, HIPAA, ERISA, CLIA, OSHA, Medicare, CMS, electronic medical records, electronic prescriptions, PQRI, licensing, contracting, credentialing, conflict resolution, purchasing, insurance laws, insurance appeal and grievance procedures, federal trade commission laws, red-flag laws, state privacy laws, advertising, marketing, malpractice, liability insurance, health insurance, employee benefits, office repair and more.

Oh yeah – they also need to know how to get along with the physician's spouse and be available as a travel agent, reservations clerk and anything else the doctor expects them to do – while making sure the practice collects enough money to pay the bills and contribute to the physician's retirement. Oh yeah – let's not forget that this super-human person must also be active in the local community since the office is represented by them, so they need to be able to do all of this while raising a family, going to church and keeping up with the physician's social calendar.

One problem that many physicians make is that they expect the act of putting a wedding ring on a spouse will magically enable a spouse to be able to do all of this. WRONG! It doesn't matter who is in this position, but they need MORE annual training than any physician needs in CMEs because they are trying to do it ALL! Insurance laws change. Fair Credit Collection laws change. So do procedure codes, coverage, diagnosis codes, privacy laws, HIPAA, CLIA, credentialing, and just about everything that I've mentioned in the previous two paragraphs. If a physician expects that knowledge to somehow be absorbed by the manager through the air without constant updates, training, networking, seminars, webinars, etc.., then they are a fool and do not deserve to be successful in their business.

For this reason, we recommend the Physician Office Manager Association of America (POMAA) and you can get more information on them at www.pomaa.net .

# HIPAA – Not HIPPA

The Health Insurance Portability & Accountability Act (HIPAA) has been around since 1996 and requires physicians to basically safeguard patient health information in their office, transmitted electronically, shared with employees, used by billing services, collection agencies, attorneys, etc...

It makes sense, although – as with any governmental requirement, they definitely get carried away with it. Remember – if the bureaucrats did not make things complex and confusing, then they wouldn't get to hire their friends, spend obscene amounts of money on compliance and ensure they have a job next year with perks and benefits.  So – they've made a mountain out of this molehill and it continues to grow, faster than the hoopla about Tiger and women.

So – where does this leave the typical medical office?  It leaves them with mounds of paperwork and restrictions on how they handle their patient data.  Fortunately, it's not as confusing – on a day to day basis – as some would have you believe.

For instance, when your patient checks in at the front window, you are allowed to have a typical patient sign-in sheet that physicians have been using since the word gay was defined as happy.

Your patient sign in sheet can have the patient's name, time they arrived and which physician they are here to see, as long as it does not disclose any financial or medical information linked to the patient's identity.  As an example, when I was in southern California to speak at the AOA convention a couple of years ago, I stopped by a family physician's office to say hello. I immediately noticed that Jose Hernandez (not his real name) was seen that morning at 8:45am because his urine had an unpleasant odor. Uh – when DOESN'T urine have an unpleasant odor? Yes – that was a HIPAA violation and as you can imagine, the physician and the office manager and I had a discussion about that very issue (and patient) before I left.

On the other hand, I've seen too many offices get carried away in compulsive –obsessive behavior to the point they made Monica from the television show FRIENDS look mellow. Some office managers are spending $34.50 for a pack of patient sign in sheets, that have a peel off label where the patient signs, so it can be removed from prying eyes.

Some are being told by salespeople selling these supplies that it is a HIPAA violation to use a typical sign in sheet, but is it really required by HIPAA? Nope. The Office for Civil Rights (OCR) (division of) Health & Human Services that oversees and enforces HIPAA clearly says on their website at: http://www.hhs.gov/ocr/privacy/hipaa/faq/providers/smaller/199.html that you can use a sign-in sheet, but that *"the sign-in sheet may not display medical information that is not necessary for the purpose of signing in"* I've also seen the question raised about whether you can call someone by their name, in the reception area.

In one office that I was visiting in south Texas, I noticed the receptionist calling patients BY NAME up to the reception window and in a not-very-quiet voice saying

"You are patient 34" and the next patient she called up was "35".

The nurse would then come out into the reception area and call patients back by number – thinking they were being HIPAA compliant.

The office manager was adamant that they had to prevent anyone from hearing another patient's name. She had been to a seminar in Austin on HIPAA by a state association. (Be careful which seminars you or your staff attend!)

I showed her on CMS' website the statement from OCR, saying "The HIPAA Privacy Rule explicitly permits the incidental disclosures that may result from this practice, for example, when other patients in a waiting room hear the identity of the person whose name is called, or see other patient names on a sign-in sheet."

This same office had invested quite a bit of money and hundreds of hours in employee time in switching the labels on EVERY patient medical chart to numbers only – so as to comply with HIPAA. They definitely had locking file cabinets (which was not inexpensive) and they had taken HIPAA to the level that made a HIPAA supply salesperson very happy.

By the way – it is not a problem if one patient sees a name of a different patient on a chart while they're walking down the hall. It is called "incidental disclosure" because it was not done intentionally and HIPAA laws are not violated in that situation.

Now, if a patient picks up someone else's chart and starts reading it – that is a problem and per the ARRA (American Recovery & Reinvestment Act of 2009, there must be breech notification. Part of the ARRA included the HITECH ACT which requires providers to update their policies on breach notification. The regulations on this went into effect last September, but sanctions can be assessed against providers as of February 22 of 2010.

It basically requires that patients be notified of certain breaches of security of their protected health information, when that breach compromises the privacy or security of the PHI.

## Breach of PHI

HIPAA defines it as: "the acquisition, access, use, or disclosure of PHI in a manner not permitted under the HIPAA privacy regulations which compromises the security or privacy of the PHI. A breach, however, does not include the following:

- any unintentional acquisition, access, or use of PHI by a workforce member or person acting under the authority of a covered entity or a business associate, if such acquisition, access, or use was made in good faith and within the scope of authority and does not result in further use or disclosure;
- any inadvertent disclosure by a person who is authorized to access PHI at a covered

entity or business associate to another person authorized to access PHI at the same covered entity or business associate; and

- a disclosure of PHI where a covered entity or business associate have a good faith belief that an unauthorized person to whom the disclosure was made would not reasonably have been able to retain such information.

So—what does it mean when it says "Compromises the privacy or security of PHI"? I've seen it said that the compromise must pose a significant risk of financial, reputational, or other harm to the individual. You've all had the classes on PHI and HIPAA by now (unless you've been stuck on an island in the pacific talking to a soccer ball for the past 7 years) but it's important that you understand what PHI is. PHI is any medical or financial information about a patient that also identifies that patient (such as their name or social or drivers license or insurance number).

So—let's say you find out that there has been a disclosure (the doc's laptop is stolen on his way home out of his car while he stopped at the hospital to make rounds). If that laptop did not have a password to open it or some other security device, a breach has likely occurred if PHI is kept on the computer. In this case, notification needs to occur to the patients that are affected.

On the other hand, if the doctor misses a turn and drives into a river and the car is submerged and the laptop floats out of the window and can't be found on the bottom of the river, then no breach likely occurred and no notification will probably be required. In the event of a breach, each individual needs to be notified within 60 days of what was possibly disclosed (numbers, names, dates, diagnosis, test results), what happened and it's a log also needs to be kept and submitted to the Department of Health & Human Services.

If the PHI involves more than 500 individuals in the breach, the Department of Health & Human Services also needs to be notified at the time of disclosure instead of waiting once a year to notify them.

It is important to note that **business associates are now also required to report any breaches to a covered entity**, so if you are a consultant or billing service covered by a BAA—you are now responsible under HITECH also. For this reason, you may want to set up additional safeguards or passwords to make "all reasonable attempts" to secure any PHI you may be in possession of.

Some office managers get carried away with making everyone (including employees) sign a Business Associate Agreement – but it's not required in certain circumstances.

For instance, a business associate contract is not required with persons or organizations whose functions, activities, or services do not involve the use or disclosure of protected health information, and where any access to protected health information by such persons would be incidental, if at all. Generally, janitorial services that clean the offices or facilities of a medical office are not business associates because the work they perform does not involve the use or disclosure of protected health information, and any disclosure of protected health information to janitorial personnel that occurs in the performance of their duties (such as may occur while emptying trash cans) is limited in nature, occurs as a by-product of their janitorial duties, and could not be reasonably prevented. Such disclosures are incidental and permitted by the HIPAA Privacy Rule.

Conversely, if you are sending claims or EOBs (Explanation of Benefits) to a consultant (such as myself) to review to make sure you're staying compliant on your coding and modifier usage, you better make sure you have a signed BAA on file in case the HIPAA Police ever ask for it.

Office managers and physicians are routinely asking whether HIPAA prohibits them from discussing the patient's care, condition, treatment or treatment options with family members or close friends.

HIPAA specifically permits physicians and clinics to share information that is directly relevant to the involvement of a spouse, family members, friends, or other persons identified by a patient. The physician may discuss this information with the family and close friends if the patient agrees or, when given the opportunity, does not object. The physician (clinic, provider, non physician provider, etc) may also share relevant information with the family and these other persons if they can reasonably infer, based on professional judgment, that the patient does not object. The problem is the way that MOST offices have worded their Notice of Patient Privacy forms. Most will word it something similar to: *"We are not allowed to disclose PHI or your health information to any family member or close friend, except for those you list below"* and then they'll have a few blanks for the patient to complete. THIS IS BACKWARDS!

It would be much better to have your Notice of Patient Privacy worded similar to: "Unless you tell us otherwise, we may share medical information about you with friends, family members, or others you have named who help with your care.

It is our policy to leave appointment schedules on your voicemail or answering system at your home as well as with family members that will answer your phone. If there are family members that you wish to restrict us talking to, it is your responsibility to list them below on the lines provided, or we will follow our standard procedure. We may use or share medical information about you with disaster organizations so that your family can be notified of your location and condition in case of disaster or other emergency."

Below is one that we picked up at an office, giving the patients the option of indicating what they authorize and which ones they do not. You're welcome to modify it for your NPP.

***Due to the HIPAA Privacy Laws, we need you to list the people that you DO NOT approve to have access to the following healthcare information: (it is our policy to speak with anyone in your household that answers the phone if we need to leave you a reminder of an appointment, ask insurance, billing or employment questions or to notify of prescription authorization unless you list them below)***

*Appointment Scheduling Information:* _____

*Billing Information:* _____

*Lab Results / Test Results:* _____

*Prescriptions / Medication information:* _____

***Authorization to Mail Postcards***    *Initials:* _____

*I authorize Dr. Feel-better to mail appointment reminder cards, test results cards and appointment cancellation cards to the address that I currently have on file at this office. This authorization will be in effect until I have given <u>written notice</u> to the office to the contrary.*

## ***Authorization to Leave Messages***
     *Initials:_____*

_I authorize Dr. Feel-better to leave messages regarding my medical condition, such as lab reports, other test results, medications, and appointment reminders on my home answering machine. This authorization will be in effect until I have given written notice to Dr. Feel-better to the contrary_

### Authorization to Contact at Employment     _Initials:_

_____

_I authorize Dr. Feel-better to leave a message reminding me of my appointment at my place of employment if they are unable to leave this message at my home number for any reason. I may revoke this authorization by giving written notice to Dr. Feel-better._

_Signature:_____

_Date:_____


# Sending PHI Overseas

While we're on the subject of HIPAA, let's also discuss the potential problems when a medical office in the U.S.A. decides to save some money on transcription costs or perhaps decides to utilize a billing service in another country.

This can be a big monthly savings in expense. It is no secret that it's less expensive to use services in India or Pakistan because their cost of living is so much less than it is here, so therefore, they can pass along the savings to the end user (you!). The problem is that HIPAA does not extend beyond the borders of America, so the federal officials cannot prosecute someone in Bangladesh the way they can prosecute someone in Tulsa. Now – we hope that everyone dealing in this business is honest – but we know that is not the case, so the question then arises whether the manager or physician wishes to assume that risk.

The risk is pretty high and should be seriously considered. If someone in India or Pakistan or Tibet (or wherever they are located) is handed PHI on your patient by your office so they can do transcription, billing, patient statements, etc..., then YOU will be held liable and culpable if THEY decide to do something that violates HIPAA with that information. They can't be prosecuted as the long arm of the US laws do not extend to their country – but you can. Now – what are those fines?

Federal law says the person convicted of violating 42 USC 1320d-6 (HIPAA Sec. 1177) in criminal court will

1. be fined not more than $50,000, imprisoned not more than 1 year, or both;
2. if the offense is committed under false pretenses, be fined not more than $100,000, imprisoned not more than 5 years, or both; and
3. if the offense is committed with intent to sell, transfer, or use individually identifiable health information for commercial advantage, personal gain, or malicious harm, be fined not more than $250,000, imprisoned not more than 10 years, or both."

Keep in mind that these are PER VIOLATION, so in effect – it is per patient that has their PHI disclosed.

The top violation that occurs with private practice clinics, per the website at: http://www.hhs.gov/ocr/privacy/hipaa/enforcement/data/top5issues.html is *"Impermissible Uses and Disclosures"*

If you're not taking HIPAA seriously yet, you should do so before someone sizes you for an orange jumpsuit!

If you have specific questions about HIPAA, it is best to visit the government website at: http://www.hhs.gov/ocr/privacy/index.html and be VERY suspicious of individuals or salespeople trying to sell you the latest "HIPAA mandated" product.

If you're in doubt of something they are trying to sell you and they tell you that it is required by HIPAA – have them show you where on the official CMS OCR website where it is required. If they cannot – then kick them to the curb and keep your wallet in your pocket.

There is so much about HIPAA that you need to learn that we cannot cover it all in this book, but you can access the website of the Health & Human Services at http://www.hhs.gov/ocr/privacy/index.html and spend days there educating yourself on it. We want to cover a few things that we see affects most medical offices:

## Patient Sign In Forms

When HIPAA came out on 1996, the word was circulating through hundreds of thousands of clinics that HIPAA prevents them from using patient sign in forms that allow others to see the patients' names by subsequent patients. Interestingly, the ones saying this the loudest were usually those people selling the $19.95 sign in forms that peel off. HIPAA does NOT prevent you from using the standard form that you've been using for years – if you wish to, as long as you do not disclose PHI (protected health information). PHI has been described as the patient's name or identifying number, along with any medical OR financial data. Just the name is not PHI.

So, you can have the patients sign in on a sheet and give what time they arrive, their name and even which physician they are seeing – and you'll still be compliant with HIPAA without spending $19.95 on a pad of forms or strips. You cannot have the patient indicate if they have insurance, if their insurance has changed, how they plan on paying for today or why they want to see the doctor – as that becomes PHI.

## Locking File Cabinets

Can you guess who has been telling physicians they must have locking file cabinets in their office to keep medical charts in, at night and when they are closed? Yes – the locking file cabinet salespeople have been very busy – and in my opinion – very naughty as well. There is no requirement by HIPAA that you have locking file cabinets in your office, in spite of what you may have heard from a salesperson.

## Calling Patients By Name

As we discussed in the first bullet, the patient's name is not HPI, by itself. Yet, we have seen offices that would assign the patient a number as they arrived and then they would call the patient by number.

This sounds much too impersonal and reminds me of something futuristic in a movie - and it is NOT required by HIPAA (as of the date this book was written). The HIPAA Privacy Rule explicitly permits the incidental disclosures that may result from calling patients to the back, for example, when other patients in a waiting room hear the identity of the person whose name is called, or see other patient names on a sign-in sheet. However, these incidental disclosures are permitted only when the covered entity has implemented reasonable safeguards and the minimum necessary standard, where appropriate.

1. NPP Length of Time:: How often does a clinic have to require the patient sign a new Notice of Patient Privacy form? A clinic or health care provider with a direct treatment relationship with patients is required to have the patient sign the NPP once, when they start seeing the patient, per 45 CFR 164.520(c)(2). If you make changes to your NPP form, then it makes sense to have the patient sign the revised one, as soon as they return to your office.

2. Audible Information Over The Phone: One person asked: "When I received my bill for a visit, it neglected to show correct insurance information. When I called and informed them that our policy had changed, they asked me to fax them a copy of my card, front and back. I didn't have a fax available that day (our fax was down), so I asked if I could read it to her over the phone.

I know the person well that I was talking to (we go to church together), but she said that HIPAA wouldn't allow giving insurance information "over the phone," and I had to fax it. Is this true?

Absolutely NOT. It is shocking how much information is believed in medical offices that is not true, ranging from HIPAA to Collection Laws to not being able to bill for this or that. HIPAA does NOT preclude you from giving information over the phone or any office from obtaining information over the phone.

3. Disclosing Medical Records from Previous Provider: Often, you will receive medical records from the patient's previous medical provider and use that data in providing care to the patient.

   If that patient moves and requests your records be forwarded to their new physician, it is perfectly legal – per HIPAA to forward ALL of the records you have – including those from the previous physician – as long as it can affect the treatment the patient may get from the new physician.

# E&M Documentation

Since more and more doctors are being audited by Medicare, Blue Cross, Tricare, Medicaid and others, it's vitally important that EVERY office be aware of some of the principles of documentation. Yes – these are basic principles – but you may be surprised at how many people how have worked in medical offices for years have no idea what these are.

1. The medical record must be complete and legible. No – when we say "legible", we are not referring to the fact that the doctor's nurse, who has worked with him for 19 years, can decipher it. Legible means the auditor can read it, without any help from the doctor or nurse (or National Security Agency cryptologist analyst). Most auditors use an unofficial "two layperson" rule in that if two laypeople can't read it – they don't count it.

2. If the reason for ordering the diagnostic tests is not documented, it must EASILY be inferred from the documentation present.

3. Past and present diagnosis should be accessible to the treating and/or consulting physician.

4. All appropriate health risk factors should be identified (not just some – but ALL)

5. The CPT and ICD-9 codes on the claim form are required to be supported by documentation in the progress notes.

6. The documentation should include the following:

   a. Reason for the encounter. (chief complaint) "Why are you here" is a question that should be asked by the nurse or aide that is taking the patient to the exam room. Terms like "follow-up" or "meds refill" is not a clear chief complaint. Why is the patient here for meds follow-up? If they are here because of their diabetes medicine, list diabetes as the chief complaint. If they are here for follow-up, then specify what condition is being followed up.

   b. Relevant history, physical exam findings and prior diagnostic test results

   c. Assessment, clinical impression of diagnosis, and

   d. Date and legible identity of the provider.

If you are still writing SOAP notes, you are probably NOT meeting the 95 or 97 guidelines. We recommend you adopt a template system or an Electronic Health Record (EHR) system.

Speaking of the 95 and 97 guidelines.... About 4 years ago, several Medicare carrier directors made announcements that they require bullets be used to identify the exam elements with the 95 guidelines. This is extremely confusing and disconcerting to certified coders around the nation. Most have believed that the "guidelines" were more than guidelines. Most have felt they were the final requirement or rule. Per CMS recently, the guidelines are not set in stone. The carriers can alter their own requirements as they deem necessary. This is not good news, but it is legal and they can do so. So, our recommendation is now that every doctor document bullets in case you get audited by Medicare.

If you need a template for documentation, you can download some at templates page by going to my website at www.donself.com and scroll down to Templates. If you find one on the page it takes you to, download it and use it and alter it if you wish. If not – make one – but make sure you document the E&M bullets. If you need additional training on this, consider sitting in on the E&M internet live webinars that we teach, using the E&M Documentation sliderule. You can also order these as well, also on my website.

## Medicare Documentation Pointers

Medicare recently published the following pointers for documentation.

- Medicare expects the documentation to be generated during the time of service or shortly thereafter.

- Delayed entries within a reasonable time frame (24-48 hrs.) are acceptable for purposes of clarification, error correction, the addition of information not initially available, and if certain unusual circumstances prevented the generation of the note at the time of service.

- The medical record cannot be altered. Errors must be legibly corrected so that the reviewer can draw an inference as to their origin. These corrections or additions must be dated, preferably timed, and legibly signed or initialed.

- Every note stands alone, i.e., the performed services must be documented at the outset.

- Delayed written explanations will be considered for purposes of clarification only. They cannot be used to add and authenticate services billed and not documented at the time of service or to retrospectively substantiate medical necessity. For that, the medical record must stand on its own with the original entry corroborating that the service was rendered and was medically necessary.

- All entries must be legible to another reader to a degree that a meaningful review can be conducted.

- All notes should be dated, preferably timed, and signed by the author.

In the office setting, initials are acceptable as long as they clearly identify the author.

- If the signature is not legible and does not identify the author, a printed version should be also recorded.

As it stands, you can and should make documentation addendums, but make sure your addendum is dated on the date you create the addendum. If an audit has already been initiated, we do not recommend you change your coding records in any way – although addenda can still be made to clarify any confusion.

While we're on the subject, we also need to make sure our patients completely understand the physician's instructions and directions.

**A woman brought the baby to see a doctor, & he determined right away that the baby had an earache, and wrote a prescription for ear drops. In the directions it was written, "Put two drops in right ear every four hours" & the word "right" was abbreviated as an R with a circle around it. Several days passed, & the woman returned with the baby, complaining that the baby still had an earache, & his little bottom was getting really greasy with all those drops of oil. The doctor looked at the bottle of ear drops & sure enough, the pharmacist had typed the following instructions on the label: "Put two drops in R ear every four hours."**

## E&M Chief Complaint:

A concise statement describing the symptom, problem, condition, diagnosis or other factor that is the reason for the encounter, usually stated in the patient's words. This can be documented by the nurse, aide, assistant or physician.

First, let's discuss WHO can document the chief complaint. Even though some seminar leaders are teaching that ONLY the physician can document the chief complaint, there is no basis for this belief in the 95 or 97 guidelines mandated by CMS and Medicare. I have never once talked to a Medicare auditor or policy official at Medicare that felt it was vital that the doctor be the one to dictate it or write it in the notes.

What IS important is that the chief complaint be clearly inferred or documented in the medical record. Without it—you may find that the visit is denied as being a routine physical or not medically necessary.

For example, I did a practice analysis for a 4 doctor Internal Medicine group. Several of the progress notes only said "Here for follow-up", so I had to see which diagnosis were actually treated, The patient had diabetes, hypertension and hyperlipidemia, so at first—I thought it would be easy to derive a chief complaint—but I was wrong. The doctor had not ordered ANY lab tests on that visit (in spite of the fact that it had been 4 months since the previous visit and we all know that Medicare wants labs on patients every 3 months when they have these conditions).

The doctor said in the notes that the patient was "at goal" on all 3 conditions and did not address them in the treatment plan.   No medications were changed or even shown they were reviewed.

The doctor did not order any diagnostics on this visit, such as ABI for the patient (1 out of every 3 patients with hypertension have P.A.D), autonomic testing due to the diabetes, holter (22% of asymptomatic diabetics have silent ischemia), etc... - so I had to advise the doctor that a Medicare auditor would probably deny the claim.

It's important to understand that a Medicare auditor will be looking for the medical necessity of not only the visit – but also whether the level of visit was commensurate with the type of problem that is affected by the chief complaint.

"Even if a "complete" note is generated, only the MEDICALLY REASONABLE AND NECESSARY SERVICES for the condition of the particular patient at the TIME OF THE ENCOUNTER AS DOCUMENTED can be considered when selecting the appropriate level of the E&M service.

Every visit code from new patient to establish patient requires a chief complaint and without one, you are probably looking at a preventive medicine visit instead of a sick visit.

Also – be aware that the chief complaint may be written as one thing by the nurse or M.A. or whomever brings the patient into the room and documents the chief complaints – but may be changed by the physician when the TRUE reason for the visit is known. You may ask if I'm implying that patients may lie from time to time, and if you are – the answer is YES. Gregory House (played by actor Hugh Laurie) routinely says that patients lie – and that part is well written – because they do. Take, for instance, the 67 year old Medicare patient that tells the medical assistant (while she is taking the vitals) that he's there to talk to the doctor about his arthritis in his right arm and may even hold it gently or cradle it like it hurts. When the physician walks into the room, he thrusts it out and shakes the doctor's hand vigorously and explains that he's really there for the little blue pills to improve his sex life.

If asked, he will explain that he couldn't be expected to "tell that young filly what I really want, as that would be embarrassing". By the way, if this happens, doctor – it is up to you to do the right thing and how you ask the question will determine whether the patient will be paying for this visit out of his pocket or whether Medicare will. If you ask him if he is having a sexual dysfunction or impotence problem and he says "no – I just want it for more opportunities to enjoy sex", then the patient will be paying for the visit in full and Medicare will not be paying a penny towards it. Medicare doesn't cover visits to ask for recreational prescriptions.

Medicare does pay for sexual dysfunction or impotence as a chief complaint or diagnosis – so you may want to make sure to ask that question of your patient. If they insist they "have no problems", then pull out the ABN (Advanced Beneficiary Notice) and have the patient sign it at the beginning of the visit.

This acknowledges that the patient will be paying for this medically unnecessary visit, as the office visit would be payable under different circumstances and an ABN is required if you wish to be paid. We'll discuss ABNs in more detail, later in this book.

## E&M HPI

While CMS officials have publicly stated that the HPI must be documented by the physician, anyone can obtain it – as long as the physician reviews and documents it. The question then arises as to what is HPI and what does each of the different elements of the HPI encompass. Here are some definitions of the elements of the HPI, and note that all of these ARE listed on the E&M Documentation sliderule on our website at https://shop.donself.com.

**Location**: Defined as a place where something is or could be located; (DUHH!) This one is REALLY easy. Most complaints refer to a specific area of the body that hurts, creaks, or has an injury, bump, or just plain isn't functioning properly. Some of the more common examples: headache, abdominal pain, sore throat, nasal congestion, knee swelling, laceration to the finger, burning in the left hand. Not every history will always state a location.

**Quality:** An inherent or distinguishing characteristic; a property. Pain may be described as dull, stabbing, sharp, radiating or throbbing. A patient that is coughing up sputum may describe the color, such as red-tinged, or green or yellow. A laceration may be described as jagged or straight, a sore throat may be described as scratchy. A headache may be described as pounding or constant.

**Severity**: The state or quality of being severe. Pain is frequently measured on a scale of 1-10, with 10 as the highest. This is an indication of the severity of the pain. You will note from the definition, that severity itself is considered a "quality". The questions one might ask is "just how bad is that scratchy throat," or you might read statements such as "he had so much trouble (with coughing and choking) that he got very frightened." On the opposite side, you may see "the patient feels really well". Severity may also be measured in comparison to previously experienced illness or injury, or even different stages of the current complaint

**Duration**: Continuance or persistence in time. How long has this problem, symptom or illness been present? Perhaps it just came on three days ago or perhaps it has been hurting for six months?

**Timing**: Regularity of recurrence: Maybe it happens every week, every month, when the weather changes, once a year, etc... The patient has nausea and vomiting in the morning. Other statements such as "seldom" or "frequently" when used to describe the regularity of the recurrence may be counted toward timing.

**Context**: The circumstances in which an event occurs; a setting Context seems to be the one descriptor that has given auditors the most trouble.

Look for statements that describe how a complaint occurred. "Injuries incurred in a freakish lawnmower racing accident", or "while I was jumping nude on the trampoline", or "flying my kite on the roof during a thunderstorm", or "yelling at the television during the world Tiddlywinks competition", or "playing the banjo outside the neighborhood Rappers bar", etc.

**Modifying Factors**: Factor is described as anything that actively contributes to or modifies the progression of the symptom, such as "it helped when I took 11 aspirin", or "the pain worsened when I would hit my head against the wall" or "I lost all feelings in my body when I stuck my tongue on the car battery" or "sitting in the hot tub made my pain go away – until my wife found out that I wasn't alone in the tub and then the pain came back". In some cases, a patient may have received care from other physicians or practitioners such as a Chiropractor or Naturalist, etc…. The treatment or care provided by these professionals may indeed be a modifying factor for today's chief complaint.

**Associated Signs and Symptoms**: A characteristic sign or indication of the existence of something else: An indication that there is a change from normal function, sensation, or appearance.

Patients who describe the scratchy throat with nasal congestion and low grade fevers, are describing not only the chief complaint, but also the associated signs and symptoms. Usually these signs and symptoms are volunteered by the patient and can be counted.

# History Of Present Illness

As everyone knows, one of the 3 basic components of an E&M is the HPI. Although it is possible to bill an established patient visit while only documenting the Exam and MDM, all 3 components are required for a new patient. Dianne Wilkinson had some fun applying song titles to the different elements of the HPI to demonstrate what each is:

- LOCATION: "All My Exes Live in Texas" (George Strait)
- SEVERITY: "I'm So Lonesome I Could Cry" (Hank Williams, Sr.)
- ASSOC.S&S: "Bewitched, Bothered, and Bewildered" (Frank Sinatra)
- CONTEXT: "Singing in the Rain" (Gene Kelly)
- TIMING: "I Go Out Walkin' After Midnight" (Patsy Cline)
- DURATION: "Endless Love" (Diana Ross/Lionel Ritchie)
- QUALITY: "Achy-Breaky Heart" (Billy Ray Cyrus)
- MODIFYING FACTORS: "D-I-V-O-R-C-E" (Tammy Wynette...something she did MORE THAN ONCE to "make it better")!!

Dianne is not only a great help in the coding world, but is also an experienced and accomplished musician and I'm blessed to call her my friend.

Since all 3 components (history, exam and medical decision making) are required for consultations (yes – non Medicare plans still pay for consultations), emergency room visits, initial inpatient hospital and initial skilled nursing visits – you need to make sure that your history is well documented on every visit as you do not know when it may be the history of present illness that results in you being down-coded or in having your level of care supported by the HPI. History consists of the HPI (History of Present Illness), Review of Systems (ROS) and PFSH (Past, Family, Social History).

## Review Of Systems (ROS)

One dictionary identifies it as a "system-by-system review of the body functions". The Review of Systems is usually begun during the history portion of the visit and completed during the examination, as the physical findings prompt additional questions.

Unlike the HPI, the ROS can be obtained and documented by anyone (per CMS, Medicare and the pointy headed auditors). In fact, many offices have the PATIENT complete a review of system form instead of having the nurse or physician do it. When you consider that the physician's time is worth more than $400 per hour (at least – that is what their time SHOULD be generating in collections), and the nurse's time is worth more than $10.00 an hour (or whatever you're paying your assistant), then it is logical to have the patient complete the form. You can download a free Symptom Survey on the donself.com website and modify it (it's in Microsoft Word and PDF) to whatever you want and then have the patients complete it as your Review of Systems.

Note – even though the patient may complete the entire form, with positives and negatives, you can only count the RELEVANT items towards the points you need for the Review of Systems. If it's not relevant - then we cannot count it towards the ROS, PFSH or even the exam, as relevancy is paramount when being audited. So, you download the form and you modify it and you have the patient complete it and you realize that you now have a patient that has marked every area with high severity and you only have a 15 minute visit – so what do you do? This is where discipline comes into necessity for the physician or non physician practitioner.

You need to explain to the patient that you'll concentrate today's visit on the chief complaint, but that you see that you need to schedule the patient for an extended 30 minute visit within the next week or so to address the other problems. This would also be a great time to pre-order the clinical lab and diagnostic tests that you'll need, so that you can use that next appointment to go over the results as well. While we're not attorneys, I have a feeling that would probably cover your medical-legal obligations when the patient brings up the fact that they are a train wreck.

Now – with this in mind, what is the requirement for Review of Systems (ROS) for each level of office visit? You'll notice in the E&M documentation requirements (also downloadable on the www.donself.com website), that the

- level 3 outpatient/office visit requires 2-9 ROS for a new patient, but only 1 Review of System for an established patient.
- A level 4 visit requires 10 ROS for a new patient, but only 2 to 9 for an established patient, and
- Level 5 office visit requires 10 (again) for a new or established patient.

The symptom survey form at www.donself.com lists the following System areas and areas within them include:

CONSITUTIONAL: fatigue, hyperactive, restless, sleepiness, insomnia, dizziness
EMOTIONAL: depression, anxiety, mood swings, irritability, forgetfulness
HEAD/EARS: headache, earache, ear infection, ringing in ears, itchy ears, discharge from ears
SKIN: blemishes, rashes, eczema, itching, rosy cheeks
NASAL/SINUS: post nasal drip, sinus pain, runny nose, stuffy nose, sneezing
MUSCULOSKELETAL: joint pains, stiff joints, aching, muscle aches, arthritis
CARDIO: irregular heartbeat, high blood pressure, intermittent chest pain, radiating left arm pain, unexplained jaw pain
DIGESTIVE: heartburn, reflux, stomach pain, cramps, constipation, diarrhea, bloating, gas, nausea, painful elimination
LOWER: leg cramps, feet numbness, tingling, legs hurt when walking, sores on legs not healing, tingling in legs, legs go to sleep

Others you may consider adding to the form, If you decide to use it, may be

SKIN: bruising, discoloration, pruritus, birthmarks, moles, ulcers, decubiti, changes in the hair or nails, sun exposure and protection.

HEMATOLOGY: spontaneous or excessive bleeding, fatigue, enlarged or tender lymph nodes, pallor, history of anemia.

HEAD AND FACE: pain, traumatic injury, ptosis.

EARS: tinnitus, change in hearing, deafness, dizziness.

EYES: change in vision, pain, inflammation, infections, double vision, scotomata, blurring, tearing.

MOUTH: dental problems, hoarseness, dysphagia, bleeding gums, ulcers or sores in the mouth.

NOSE and sinuses discharge, epistaxis, obstruction.

BREASTS: pain, change in contour or skin color, lumps, discharge from the nipple.

RESPIRATORY: tract cough, sputum, change in sputum, night sweats, nocturnal dyspnea, wheezing.

CARDIOVASCULAR: chest pain, dyspnea, palpitations, weakness, intolerance of exercise, varicosities, swelling of extremities, known murmur, hypertension, asystole.

GASTROINTESTINAL: nausea, vomiting, diarrhea, constipation, quality of appetite, change in appetite, dysphagia, gas, heartburn, melena, change in bowel habits, use of laxatives or other drugs to alter the function of the gastrointestinal tract.

URINARY: dysuria, change in color of urine, change in frequency of urination, pain with urgency, incontinence, edema, retention, nocturia.

genital tract (female) menstrual history, obstetric history, contraceptive use, discharge, pain or discomfort, pruritus, history of venereal disease, sexual history.

GENITAL: (male) penile discharge, pain or discomfort, pruritus, skin lesions, hematuria, history of venereal disease, sexual history.

SKELETAL: heat; redness; swelling; limitation of function; deformity; crepitation: pain in a joint or an extremity, the neck, or the back, especially with movement.

NERVOUS SYSTEM: dizziness, tremor, ataxia, difficulty in speaking, change in speech, paresthesia, loss of sensation, seizures, syncope, changes in memory.

ENDOCRINE: tremor, palpitations, intolerance of heat or cold, polyuria, polydipsia, polyphagia, diaphoresis, exophthalmos, goiter.

PSYCHOLOGIC: nervousness, instability, depression, phobia, sexual disturbances, criminal behavior, insomnia, night terrors, mania, memory loss, perseveration, disorientation.

Remember that you will not be penalized for documenting too much – but you can definitely be penalized for not documenting enough.

# ROS – Non Contributory

"All ROS non contributory" does not give us the ROS needed to support a level 3, 4 or 5 visit. This was recently supported in a letter by a Medicare medical director, who said: "Bogus histories and physicals are created in one of 6 ways.

1. A physician will dictate (or write) under family history, social history, or review of systems, the word, "non-contributory," although he/she never asked any questions about these components.

2. If there is a transcription service, the transcriber will type "non-contributory," even though nothing was dictated.

3. Voice recognition computer programs will either add "noncontributory" or even create "negative/normal" as

descriptions for physical findings that were also not mentioned.

4. "WNL" for "Within Normal Limits" will be noted (unfortunately, this usually stands for "We Never Looked").

5. A physician may use a "canned" dictation:

6. A physician may abuse the cutting and pasting functions of word processors to create "documentation."

These nonexistent histories and physicals are a problem:

- First, it is pathetic medical care that will not accurately reflect what the patient's true condition was on the date of service, and
- Second, the services being billed were not done. so this is rightfully considered fraud by every auditor that would ever look at it.

# Symptom Survey

## SYMPTOM SURVEY

Patient Name:_____ Date:_____

Instructions: Start with the first symptom and ask yourself, "over the last 6 months, have I experienced this symptom?" If you answer no or almost not at all, then mark a "0". If the answer is yes, then ask yourself if you experience the symptom occasionally (less than 2 times in a week) or frequently (2 or more times in a week). Ask yourself if the symptom is "Severe" or "Not Severe". Using the SCALE OF SYMPTOM POINTS listed below, write the appropriate score in the corresponding field for EVERY symptom listed.

### SCALE OF SYMPTOM POINTS:

0 = Do Not Suffer From This Ever or Almost Ever
1 = Suffer OCCASIONALLY (< 2 times p/week), is not severe

2 = Suffer FREQUENTLY (2 or more times p/week), not severe
3 = Suffer OCCASSIONALLY and is severe
4 = Suffer FREQUENTLY and is severe

**CONSTITUTIONAL**
_____ Fatigue (sluggish, tired)
_____ Hyperactive (nervous energy)
_____ Restless (can't relax/sit still)
_____ Sleepiness During Day
_____ Insomnia at Night
_____ Dizziness

**EMOTIONAL/MENTAL**
_____ Depression
_____ Anxiety (vague fears, uneasiness)
_____ Mood Swings (rapid distinct changes)
_____ Irritability
_____ Forgetfulness

**HEAD/EARS**
_____ Headache (any kind)
_____ Earache
_____ Ear Infection
_____ Ringing in Ear
_____ Itchy Ears
_____ Discharge From Ears

**SKIN**
_____ Blemishes, Acne
_____ Rashes, Hives
_____ Eczema
_____ "Rosy" Cheeks

**NASAL/SINUS**
_____ Post Nasal Drip
_____ Sinus Pain
_____ Runny Nose
_____ Stuffy Nose
_____ Sneezing

**MUSCULOSKELETAL**
_____ Joint Pains/Aching
_____ Stiff Joints
_____ Muscle Aches
_____ Stiff Muscles
_____ Arthritis (Diagnosed)

**CARDIOVASCULAR**
_____ Irregular Heartbeat
_____ High Blood Pressure

**DIGESTIVE**
_____ Heartburn/Esoph.Reflux
_____ Stomach Pains/Cramps
_____ Intestinal Pains/Cramps
_____ Constipation
_____ Diarrhea
_____ Bloating Sensation
_____ Gas (of Any Kind)
_____ Nausea, Vomiting
_____ Painful Elimination

**WEIGHT MANAGEMENT**
_____ Approximate Weight
_____ Approximate Height
_____ Fluctuating Weight

**OTHER**
_____ Leg Cramp when sitting
_____ Feet get cold or numb
_____ Legs hurt walking a lot
_____ Sores - legs not healing
_____ Tingling in the legs
_____ Sleeping Difficulties

Please circle the following symptoms (if any) that you may experience or have experienced in the past 60 days:

Dizziness, Light Headedness, "weak spells", fainting, "Pounding in the chest", Palpitations, Fluttering or Flip Flop, Chest Pain, Tightness, Heaviness in the Chest, Indigestion-Like Pain, Shortness of Breath, Sensations of Choking, Intermittent Jaw Pain, Tingling Arm, Back Pain Between Shoulder Blades, Wheezing

| | | | |
|---|---|---|---|
| 1. | Have any of your immediate family members had heart disease? | [ ]YES | [ ]NO |
| 2. | Have any of your immediate family members had diabetes? | [ ]YES | [ ]NO |
| 3. | Have you recently started or stopped smoking? | [ ]YES | [ ]NO |
| 4. | Have you recently started an exercise program? | [ ]YES | [ ]NO |
| 5. | Have you fallen in the last year due to dizziness or vertigo? | [ ]YES | [ ]NO |
| 6. | Have you gotten dizzy after standing up quickly on multiple occasions? | [ ]YES | [ ]NO |

Patient Sign:_____ Date:_____

Physician Sign:_____

There are four advantages of using the Symptom Survey form from www.donself.com and having EVERY patient complete the form on EVERY VISIT (new & established).

1. You obtain enough ROS to support t the level you accurately billed, in case you're ever audited,

2. You learn more about your patient than you would normally learn by asking questions, because you will forget questions once in a while. I'm fond of saying that there have only been two men who ever walked on water and one of them sank. This implies that there was only one perfect man and that was Jesus. Every one of the rest of us humans will make mistake (if you doubt that you do – just ask your spouse). During a normal visit, the physician may have 6 to 9 minutes face to face with the patient and they will forget to ask or note or document something on just about every patient. When they are seeing that patient, they are not thinking ONLY of that patient, but also of the last patient who just left and about whether they have a pharmaceutical rep bringing lunch today. They're also considering whether their son's school play is this Thursday or is it next Thursday.

At the same time, they're thinking whether the office manager made the hotel reservation for next week's medical conference, etc... They have so much on their mind, that a physician will almost never ask all of the questions they should – because they are just human.

By having the form completed by the patient, you'll definitely learn more about the patient than if you're just asking questions.

3. The third reason is that you will see that many of your patients have the medical necessity that necessitates you ordering some diagnostic and clinical tests – and that is a good thing. Since the reimbursement for many diagnostic tests and just about every clinical lab test have been increasing every year since 2001 (while many procedures have seen decreases), it helps the practice when the physician is ordering diagnostic and clinical tests as they should – if the practice is smart enough to be doing many of them in-house. There is a true financial benefit to the patients completing these forms, resulting in the practice increasing income by performing medically necessary testing in the clinic.

Better medical care is achieved in a couple of ways. One is that the physician is screening for what could appear to be asymptomatic problems today, because not all patients will remember to bring up problems as they are in your office that could indicate something more serious. The second part of this is that the tests that will be run due to the medical necessity will allow the physician to identify and treat possible severe problems that are being missed by other physicians. For instance, per the National Institute of Health, (publication 06-5835), 33% of patients over 50 with heart disease have Peripheral Artery Disease as well. The problem is that most primary care physicians and other specialists are missing the symptoms and not diagnosing the P.A.D. until the patient has to have an amputation. Even the PQRI (126) states "in people with diabetes, 22.8% have foot problems including amputations and numbness compared to 10% of non-diabetics. It also says "Over the age of 40 years old, 30% of people with diabetes have loss of sensation in their feet".

So – by routinely asking your patients about numbness, tingling, burning, coldness in their feet, etc... on the survey – you may be helping to capture P.A.D. early enough in it's progression that you can save a toe, a foot or even a life.

## Re-Read Your Documentation

Even though you may have meant one thing, it may not hurt to occasionally re-read your documentation to make sure it doesn't appear that you meant something else. Here are some newspaper headlines to give you an idea:

- ➢ Include Your Children when Baking Cookies
- ➢ Police Begin Campaign to Run Down Jaywalkers
- ➢ Safety Experts Say School Bus Passengers Should Be Belted
- ➢ Drunk Gets Nine Months in Violin Case
- ➢ Survivor of Siamese Twins Joins Parents
- ➢ Iraqi Head Seeks Arms
- ➢ Prostitutes Appeal to Pope
- ➢ Panda Mating Fails; Veterinarian Takes Over
- ➢ British Left Waffles on Falkland Islands
- ➢ Teachers Strike Idle Kids
- ➢ Clinton Wins on Budget, But More Lies Ahead
- ➢ Enraged Cow Injures Farmer With Ax

> ➢ Miners Refuse to Work after Death
> ➢ Juvenile Court to Try Shooting Defendant
> ➢ Stolen Painting Found by Tree
> ➢ Two Sisters Reunited After 18 Years in Checkout Counter
> ➢ Killer Sentenced to Die for Second Times in 10 Years
> ➢ Never Withhold Herpes Infection from Loved One
> ➢ Red Tape Holds Up New Bridges
> ➢ Man Struck By Lightning Faces Battery Charge
> ➢ New Study of Obesity Looks for Larger Test Group
> ➢ Astronaut Takes Blame for Gas in Spacecraft
> ➢ Kids Make Nutritious Snacks
> ➢ Arson Suspect Held in Massachusetts Fire
> ➢ Ban On Soliciting Dead in Trotwood
> ➢ Local High School Dropouts Cut in Half
> ➢ Hospitals are Sued by 7 Foot Doctors

# Past, Family, Social History (PFSH)

A patient's past history is pretty self explanatory, but should usually include relevant previous surgeries, injuries, illnesses, or treatments.

Family History should include a review of medical events in the patient's family that may includes significant data about the health status of the immediate family members (parents, siblings, and children) or their cause of death of specific diseases related to problems identified in the chief complaint or history of the present illness, and/or diseases of family members which may be hereditary or place the patient at risk.

A social history is expected to include a review of past and current activities that includes relevant information about marital status, current or past employment, use of drugs including alcohol, and tobacco, diet or exercise habits, level of education, sexual history; and other relevant social factors.

Remember that each progress note stands alone, so it is not advisable for a physician or practitioner to notate "reviewed PFSH" as that doesn't give the auditor any help in crediting the provider for the PFSH elements.

Why not have your nurses or medical assistants or whomever it is that takes the patient into the exam room and gets the vitals to ask every patient (if you're not going to use the Symptom Survey) a couple of relevant PFSH questions, such as:

- Have any of your family members had heart disease?
- Have any of your family members had diabetes?
- Have you recently started an exercise program or diet?
- Have you recently stopped smoking and threatened others with a sharp object?
- Is anyone else in your family crazy or nutty as a loon?

By asking these questions, you'll be gaining information that may or may not relevant to their chief complaint or medical decision making, so we recommend you get your staff accustomed to asking.

It is important to note that in order to count them towards the PFSH, the questions need to be relevant to the problems that you are treating today or that you are taking into consideration for therapy or medical management. For instance, family questions could include completely non relevant or significant data, such as "how many children does your second cousin have". While that is not relevant, perhaps if the patient is found to have some kind of pulmonary problem, a relevant one may be "Does anyone else in your parent's immediate family such as their sisters or brothers have any history of pulmonary dysfunction?" As an example, in our family, I was unaware that my mother probably died from Pulmonary Fibrosis instead of COPD, and to most – that may not seem like a big thing, since either way, she is gone.

But – where it may become a big thing to know the extended family history is if your family has something that turns out to be genetic, such as the fact that every one of her 6 siblings may have or had the same thing and it has prematurely killed many of them already.
Now – the relevance comes in for the PFSH as that has a very likely chance on affecting myself and my children as well as my grandchildren. Would your physician think to ask that question of aunts and uncles? I don't know – but perhaps they should, and that can make a difference between mediocre and good medical care.

## Exam Body Areas

There are 10 body areas that can be examined, including:

| | |
|---|---|
| Head | Neck |
| Chest | Abdomen |
| Genital/Buttocks | Back |

Extremity

Ok, you're thinking "Don said ten, but there are only 7, so perhaps he's hit his head a few too many times?" Some of your patients may come in with only 1, 2 or 3 extremities, but if they come in with 4 – then you have 10 body areas that can be examined, as each extremity examined gets counted.

## Exam Elements:

Ok – this is the fun area. You have lots of elements that can be counted and if you are using a template (which is legal, per CMS, HHS and all of the other agencies designated with 3 letters), then you should count each element that is indicated with "Within Normal Limits" individually. (What does Don mean when he says "individually"?) If you are using a template, you must mark each area independently and not just draw a line through several elements as normal or WNL or CMS auditors (and others too, I presume) will not allow credit for those elements.

ELEMENTS: **Constitutional**:1.Appearance 2(Any three)  a-Temp  b-BP
c-Pulse d-Resp e-Wght  f-Hgt    **Eye** 1.Lids&Conj 2.Iris&Pupil
3.Opthalmoscopy, **ENT**: 1Ext ear&nose 2Ext.aud.canal & Tympanum
3Hearing 4Inner nose 5Lips,gums,teeth
6Oropharynx/mucosa/salivary/ tongue  /tonisls/ hard&softpalate,
**Neck**: 1Appearance/ Symmetry/Mass 2Thyroid. **Resp**: Effort
2Palpation 3Percuss 4Auscult, **CVS**: 1Palpitation 2Auscult 3CarotidA
4AbdA 5FemA 6PedalA 7Ext.edema/varicos. Breast: 1Appearance
2Palpation+axilla. **G.I**: 1Mass/.tender 2Liver&spleen
3Perineum/anus/rectum 4Hernia 5Hemoccult **Genitourinary male:**
1Penis 2Scrotal contents 3Prostate. **Female:** 1Ext Gen. 2Urethra 3Cervix
4Adnexa 5Uterus 6Bladder. **Lymphatics:** 1Neck 2Axilla 3Groin 4Other.
**Musculosk:** 1Gait&Station 2Inspection/palpation digists+nails
3Head&neck 4RUE 5LUE 6Spine/ribs/pelvis 7LLE 8RLE. (*Insp/Palp.
*ROM. *Stability *Power/tone **Skin:** 1Inspection 2Palpation. **Neuro:**
1C.Ns 2Sensation 3DTRs/path reflexes **Psych:** 1Insight, judgement
2Orientation 3Mood/affect 4Recent/remote memory

The very first element area listed is Constitutional and
the first one within that area is Appearance.    This
would normally be "tired, fatigued, in pain, upset, no
apparent distress (NAD), energetic, wired, cranky,
irritable, excited, angry, ecstatic, etc....

We do NOT recommend you use the words "fat" or "ugly"
as the HIPAA laws allow the patient to request to see
their own records anytime they wish, and we're already
having   enough   problems   with   patients   not
understanding   the   abbreviation   for   "Shortness   of
Breath" and we do not want to add to the problems.

After appearance, we have the vitals listed, so three
vitals – such as "temp, bp, weight" would count as one
exam element.    If they documented height, respiration
and pulse, I believe most auditors would give them
credit for a second element as well – but if they do not
document at least 3 – you don't get any element for
vitals.

With this in mind, why not have your nurse or whomever is getting the vitals to get all six vitals on every patient visit, as well as the appearance? The other elements do not take a lot of documentation, and sometimes (if they are within normal limits), it may only take a simple checkmark on a template. Conversely, if the element is NOT within normal limits, you HAVE to write, type or dictate what is abnormal, scary, missing, inflamed, enlarged, reduced, odd, freakish, grotesque, odorous, weird, or just plain... not normal so that the person reading it is very clear as to what YOU saw.

By now, I shouldn't have to point out that the TRUE benefit of documentation is not the auditors or payment or to satisfy the pointy headed money people. The real reason we do it is so that a healthcare professional will be able to make their medical decisions in the future based on what you observed or what you treated or what conclusions you came to.

Sometimes – that future healthcare provider will be you looking at your own records and it will help you in how you care for the patient. So- the more information you document, the more accurate it will be.

Overall, it shouldn't take a physician more than a minute or two to document a typical 99213 or 99214 and less than 4 minutes to document a typical 99215 if they are truly smart about how they do it. Of course, after getting a good Electronic Medical Record, it may take less time than they realize.

# Medical Decision Making

Just as the History component requires 3 parts or components (HPI, ROS & PFSH), the MDM also requires 3 distinct components.

Two of the three components determine the final level of MDM complexity documented in a record of E/M service.

> ➤ Number of diagnoses &/or management options.
> ➤ Amount and/or complexity of data reviewed or ordered.
> ➤ Risk of complication and/or mortality.

# Number of Diagnosis &/or Management Options:

*NUMBER OF DIAGNOSES :   A "problem" is defined as definitive diagnosis or, for undiagnosed problems, a related group of presenting symptoms and/or clinical findings.*

1 Point:  Each new or established problem for which the diagnosis and/or treatment plan is evident <u>with or without diagnostic confirmation</u>

2 Points:   2 plausible differential diagnoses, comorbidities or complications (not counted as separate problems) clearly stated and supported by information in record: requiring diagnostic evaluation or confirmation

3 Points:   3 plausible differential diagnoses, comorbidities or complications (not counted as separate problems) clearly stated and supported by information in record: requiring diagnostic evaluation or confirmation

4 Points: 4 or more plausible differential diagnoses, comorbidities or complications (not counted as separate problems) clearly stated and supported by information in record: requiring diagnostic evaluation or confirmation

Total Points = _____

## Management Options

Often, a provider will write "continue same therapy" or "no change in therapy". Unfortunately, most carriers will not allow this, as it doesn't indicate to the auditor what the current therapy is nor that the physician reviewed it). A record should be able to stand on it's own and usually, when a carrier or auditor requests a patient's records, it is for specific dates, so those dates have to tell them what you need them to know.
Examples of Management Options

- <4 new or current meds – p/prob = 1 point: Drug mgmnt: Incl. "same" therapy or "no change" in therapy

- >3 new or current meds – p/prob = 2 points Drug mgmnt: Incl. "same" therapy or "no change" in therapy

Note: (progress record needs to reflect active intentional decision-making to make no dose changes in order to count for coding purposes)

- 1 pt - Open or perc. therapeutic cardiac, surgical or radiological procedure; minor or major

- 1 pt - Physical, occupational or speech therapy or other manipulation
- 1 pt - Closed treatment for fracture or dislocation
- 1 pt - Conservative measures such as rest, ice/heat, specific diet, etc.
- 1 pt - Radiation therapy
- 1 pt - Joint, body cavity, soft tissue, etc injection/aspiration
- 1 pt - Patient education regarding self or home care
- 1 pt - Decision to admit to hospital
- 1 pt - Discuss case with other physician

TOTAL POINTS: _____

# Data Reviewed and/or Ordered

1-3 = 1 PT, 4 or More = 2 Pts

- ___ Clinical Lab
- ___ Diagnostic Imaging
- ___ Diagnostic Testing

- ___ (1 pt) Counsel with or discuss patient test results with performing physician
- ___ (1 pt) Discuss with other physician
- ___ (1 pt) Order &/or review. old records without summarization.
- ___ (2 pt) Order &/or review old record with a summary
- ___ (1 pt) Independent Visual interpretation of image/test/lab not reported for separate payment

TOTAL POINTS: _____

# Risk of Complications and/or Morbidity or Mortality

This area considers:

- **Presenting Problem (PP)**
- **Diagnostic Procedures Ordered (DPO)**
- **Management Options Chosen (MOC)**

## Minimal:

- PP –            One self limited or minor problem (cold, splinter in finger, insect bite, tinea corporis)
- DPO -
  - EKG,
  - Lab tests requiring venipuncture,
  - chest x-rays,
  - Urinalysis,
  - Echo Doppler
- MOC -
  - Dressings (superficial),
  - Ace Wrap,
  - gargles,
  - rest

## Low:

- PP -    2 or more self-limited/minor problems,
  - One stable chronic illness,
  - Acute uncomplicated injury or illness (allergy or simple sprain)
- DPO –
  - Skin biopsies,
  - clinical lab necessitating arterial draw, needle biopsies,
  - non-cardio imaging w/contrast,
  - PFT, etc.

- MOC –
  - Non Prescription Medications
  - Physical Therapy
  - IV Fluids (simple)
  - Minor surgery w/o risk factors

## Moderate

- PP –
  - One or more chronic illnesses with minor problems
  - Two or more stable chronic illnesses
  - Undiagnosed new problem with differential diagnosis
  - Acute Illness with systemic symptoms
  - Acute complicated injury (head wound with brief loss of consciousness)

- DPO
  - Stress Tests
  - Diagnostic endoscopies w/o risk
  - Incisional Biopsy
  - Arteriogram, cardiac cath
  - Lumbar puncture
  - Thoracentesis
  - Culdocentesis

- MOC
  - Minor surgery w identified risk factors
  - Elective surgery w/o risk factors
  - Prescription Drug Management
  - Nuclear Medicine (therapeutic)
  - IV Fluids with additives

- o   Closed treatment of fracture w/o manipulation

## High

- PP –
  - o   1 or more chronic illnesses with severe exacerbation, progression or side effects
  - o   Acute or chronic illness or injuries that may pose a threat to life or body function
  - o   Abrupt change in neurologic status

- DPO
  - o   Diagnostic endoscopies with identified risk
  - o   Cardio imaging with contrast and identified risk factors
  - o   Discography

- MOC
  - o   Decision Not to Resuscitate
  - o   Decision to de-escalate care due to poor prognosis
  - o   Emergency Major Surgery
  - o   Drug Therapy requiring intensive toxicity monitoring
  - o   Elective major surgery

Level of Risk:_____

## MDM Calculation

| DX/Mgmt | 1 pt = Min. | 2 pt = Ltd | 3 pt = Mult. | 4 pt = Exten |
|---|---|---|---|---|
| Data Rvwd/Ordered | <= 1 pt = Minimal | 2 pts = Ltd | 3 pt = Mult | 4 pt = Exten |
| Risk | Minimal | Low | Moderate | High |
| MDM | Minimal | Low | Moderate | High |

Now that you have the MDM calculated, you can select your E&M Level, based on:

New Patient:  History, Exam & MDM
Established Pt:  (2 of 3) History, Exam & MDM

# Evaluation & Management Sliderule:

A tool that more than a few people in the country have taken advantage of, for the past 10 years, is the E&M Documentation Sliderule, that is small enough to fit in a provider's pocket.

These tools help simplify the documentation requirements of the 1995 and 1997 guidelines as published by the CMS (at the time they came out, CMS was called HCFA or the Health Care Financing Administration).

They are a simple double-sided sleeve with a double-sided insert that slides in and out and have the requirements for the following categories:

- New Outpatient Visits
- Established Outpatient Visits
- Office Consultations
- Emergency Department Visits
- Initial In-patient Care (Admits)
- Follow-up Hospital Care
- Initial In-patient Consultations
- SNF Visits

You can purchase them at www.donself.com or on our shop at shop.donself.com

Don Self & Associates – www.donself.com – (903) 882-4023

|  | 99215 | 99214 | 99213 | 99212 | 99211 | Level |
|---|---|---|---|---|---|---|
| | 5 | 4 | 3 | 2 | 1 | |
| LEVEL | | | | | | |
| CHIEF COMPLAINT | Y | Y | Y | Y | Y | cc |
| History CHRONIC ILLNESS | ≥4 / ≥3 | ≥4 / ≥3 | 1-3 | 1-3 | 1-3 | HPI |
| R.O. SYSTEMS | >10 | 2-9 | 1 | – | – | ROS |
| PAST/FAMILY/SOC. HISTORY | 2 | 1 | – | – | – | PFSH |
| Exam 97 ELEMENTS | 9 / 18 / 28 / 18 | 2-6 / 12 / 2-7 / 12 | ≥1 / ≥6 / 2-7 / ≥6 | ≥1 / 1-5 / ≥1 / 1-5 | – | 97 exam |
| Exam 95 | High | Moderate | Low | Minimal | – | 95 exam |
| RISK/COMPLEXITY/(TIME) | High | Moderate | Low | Minimal | – | MDM |
| Time | 40 | 25 | 15 | 10 | 5 | Time |

2/3 ESTABLISHED OUTPATIENT

Location • Duration • Severity • Quality • Associations • Modifying Factors • Timing • Context

Constitutional • Eye • ENT • CVS • Resp • Allergic • G.I • G.U. Skin • Neuro • Psych • Endo • Heme • Mskel. • All Others Neg

**PMHx:** Ops/Illness/Meds. **FamHx:** Hereditary illness. **SocHx:** Marital, Work, ETOH, Tobacco, Drugs.

**Systems:** As ROS, **Body areas:** Head • Neck • Chest • Abdomen • Genital/buttocks • Back • Extremity

**ELEMENTS: Constitutional:** 1Appearance 2Jaundiced 3(any three) a-Temp b-BP? c-BP? d-Pulse e-Resp f-Wght g-Hgt. **Eye:** 1Lids&Conj 2Pupil/Papil 3Ophthalmoscopy. **ENT:** 1Ext ear&nose 2Ext.and canal & Tympanum 3Hearing 4Inner nose 5Lips,gums,teeth 6Oropharynx/mucosa/salivary/ tongue/tonsils/hard&softpalate. **Neck:** 1Appearance/Symmetry/Mass 2Thyroid. **Resp:** 1Effort 2Palpation 3Percuss 4Auscult. **CVS:** 1Palpation 2Auscult 3Carotid A 4AbdA 5FemA 6PedalA 7Ext edema/varices. **Breast:** 1Appearance 2Palpation+axilla. **G.I.:** 1Mass/tender 2Liver&spleen 3Perineum/anus/rectum 4Hernia 5Heme/occult. **Genitourinary male:** 1Penis 2Scrotal contents 3Prostate. **female:** 1Ext. Gen. 2Urethra 3Cervix 4Adnexa 5Uterus 6Bladder. **Lymphatics:** 1Neck 2Axilla 3Groin 4Other. **Musculosk:** 1Gait&Station 2Inspection/palpation digits+nails 3Head&neck 4RUE 5LUE 6Spine/rib/pelvis 7LLE 8RLLE. **(?)sing/Pain:** *ROM, *Stability, *Power/tone). **Skin:** 1Inspection 2Palpation. **Neuro:** 1CN.s 2Sensation 3DTR/path reflexes. **Psych:** 1Insight, judgement 2Orientation 3Mood/affect 4Recent/remote memory.

# EMR

## Incentives

You may hear (usually from a salesperson selling Electronic Health Records software) that you need to sign up for E.H.R. today because the earlier you sign up—the more you get in bonus. That is not exactly true. The first year that will count towards a bonus will be 2011. In fact—the following is from CMS' website:

· The Recovery Act establishes financial incentives beginning in January 2011 for eligible professionals (EPs) who are meaningful EHR users. Beginning in 2015, payment adjustments will be imposed on EPs who are not meaningful EHR users.

· Hospital-based physicians who substantially furnish their services in a hospital setting are not eligible.

So – as long as you have your EMR system in place and you're using it in 2011, you should be able to qualify for the bonus – so take your time to pick the RIGHT one and don't just grab one because it looks good or the salesperson is giving you a SPECIAL DEAL today.

((Employment application blanks always ask 'who is to be notified in case of an emergency.' I think we should write, "A Good Doctor!"))

## EMR Incentive Payments

The rumors abound regarding the EMR incentive payments and when physicians will be fined for not having electronic medical records. CMS has stated, on their website:

> "The incentive payment is equal to 75 percent of Medicare allowable charges for covered services furnished by the EP in a year, subject to a maximum payment in the first, second, third, fourth, and fifth years of $15,000; $12,000; $8,000; $4000; and $2,000, respectively. For early adopters whose first payment year is 2011 or 2012, the maximum payment is $18,000 in the first year.
> - There will be no payments for meaningful EHR use after 2016.
> - There would be no payments to EPs who first become meaningful EHR users in 2015 or thereafter.
> - For EPs who predominantly furnish services in a health professional shortage area (HPSA), incentive payments would be increased by 10 percent."

Now, if you're looking for a system—that's a good thing—but it is more important that you get one that will do what you need it to do to truly benefit you than to get the wrong one so as to get the little 2% bonus.

## EMR – True Benefit

Everyone is in a mad rush looking at all of the different Electronic Medical Records (or Electronic Health Records) as a way to get another bonus.

I'm not saying that the $1500 a month ($18,000 for the first year) bonus is nothing – but let's put it into perspective. Most offices are open 22.5 working days a month, so $1,500 a month equates out to $66.00 a day.

A GOOD EMR that has the right capabilities and functionality should easily increase most primary care offices by 10 times that $66 a day. Yes – a good one, when used properly should easily help most primary care offices increase their actual collections by at least $700 a day over what they were getting before going EMR.

Time is an enemy to a non efficient office and a friend to one who has learned to be as professional as they can be. EMRs can greatly reduce the time a physician and the staff spends on documentation, thereby freeing them up for patient care. At first, though, you may find it takes a bit longer until you become used to the system. In fact, in some offices, they compare the first few months on an EMR to what they think eternity will be like for people who have not accepted Jesus during the time they have on this earth.

After talking to hundreds of people who have gone through an EMR transition, I think the main reason that most offices have such a long transition period is because some was either under-estimating how much training they SHOULD get with the new system or the practice administrator was too cheap to pay for the amount of training they should get. This is probably another one of those instances where spending a nickel to make a dollar didn't happen because someone was trying to save that nickel and they took the minimum amount of training they could get.

That happens much more often than not when people are getting a new practice management or a new electronic medical record system.

Readability of the records is extremely high in our list of reasons why we like EMRs. There is no doubt at all that some clients will suffer irreparable financial harm if their records are ever audited—especially by a federal auditor, the OIG or Medicare, simply because the auditor cannot read their progress notes – and that is a very preventable error! There are some physicians arrogant or foolish enough to think that if they are audited and the auditor cannot read their record, that the auditor will take the time to call the physician or the physician's nurse to ask what it says – and they get such an education when that doesn't happen and they have to refund tens of thousands of dollars due to illegible records.

Others believe that if they are ever audited, they can take a pen to the records that are missing key ingredients to meet the level of service billed, prior to sending the records to the auditors and that too is NOT allowed and will definitely encourage the auditors to look for fraud.

Either do your documentation right the first time or don't bill above the level of legible documentation that you record. It is really that simple.

Patient care is probably the one area that is the most important when it comes to reasons why you should go EMR. A properly designed system will use the Rules (protocols) and Schedules parts of any GOOD EMR system.

The schedules should flag a patient's account and even generate a reminder for the staff when it is time for a patient to have a CBC, A1C, ABI, bone density, mammogram, pap, digital rectal exam, flu shot, etc... if you are still relying on the physician to know when it's time for the patient to have this—you are not only losing $10,000 per month—but you're endangering your patient's care needlessly. You're missing things and that may be costing your patient much more than it costs you.

The rules section of any GOOD EMR will allow you to set up the medical director's plan of care per illness so that each doctor, mid level and non physician clinical personnel will know and act on the director's care plan. For instance, if you have an ANSAR in your practice—then you know how valuable it is diagnostically to your diabetic—hypertensive patients. You can set the rule to automatically flag an ANS reminder when a patient is diagnosed with those 2 diagnoses. If the patient's A1C is above 9—then it flags an A1C should be obtained on EVERY visit the patient is in. If the patient is on long term meds, it should flag that a CBC should be obtained at least quarterly—but more often if blood sugar is above 120, or if the A1C is above 9 or if the blood pressure is above 140. We like EMRs—but not just because they help reduce paper storage or help the physician pick the appropriate level of E&M code.

When (not "if") you pick out an EMR system, you want to intentionally tell the salesperson or installer scheduler that you need EXTRA time to be spent solely on the Protocols (some call it Health Maintenance) or Rules area as that is not usually concentrated on by the EMR companies when they're training you.

The reason is simple. Those that have a good Rules and Protocol application in their system do not usually get ASKED to spend the time on it since more than 90% of the physicians and clinics in this country are not using it.

That reminds me of having a built in GPS in your car and you insist on stopping to ask directions instead of turning the GPS on.

Now, once you get the EMR scheduled, you want to make sure you visit the current PQRI listing put out by Medicare (www.donself.com) , visit the AHRQ (Agency for Healthcare Research & Quality) website (www.ahrq.gov) , check out the Medicare NCDs (National Coverage Databases) on the CMS website (www.hhs.cms.gov) and get the latest "gold standards" and use those when setting up the parameters for the rules and protocols, INSTEAD OF the way the physician has always done it.

## Mediocre Care

When you ask physicians how often they order CBCs and A1Cs and Liver Panels and ABIs and Holters and the rest of the diagnostic and lab tests, you get such a wide variety. Usually, someone will tell me "I've been doing it that way for 15 years and it's worked for me". OK – maybe it's worked for YOU – but it ISN'T working for your patients.

We are NOT doing the kind of job taking care of our patients that we should be, or we wouldn't have these kinds of numbers:

- 33% of diabetics over 50 have P.A.D. (NIH 06-5835)

- 33% of heart disease pts over 50 have P.A.D. (NICH 06-5835)

- 25% of black people over 50 have PAD (NIH 06-5835)

- 20% of Americans over 50 have P.A.D.(NIH 06-5835)

- COPD is the 4th largest killer of Americans (NIH)

- **COPD** is expected to be the 3rd-leading cause of death in the U.S. by 2020 (NIH)

- 21% of American adults have pulmonary dysfunction

- 22% of asymptomatic diabetics have silent ischemia (ADA 6/2008)

- 65% of diabetics will die from heart disease/stroke (NIH)

- Americans with COPD is expected to increase by 34.5 percent by 2013 (NIH)

- Over 60% of people with diabetes have hypertension. (ADA)

- 31% of referrals from primary care to cardiologists are due to non cardiology problems (jacc.2004.05.16)

- Falls among people 65 & older is now the leading cause of injury deaths (CDC 5/2008)

- 1 in 3 Geriatric Americans fall each year (CDC 3/2008)

These are the kinds of numbers that we've been achieving by having physicians try to remember in their heads when something needs to be done and when it doesn't.

I am fond of a saying that goes: "There has only been 2 men that walked on water, and one of them sank". Physicians CANNOT remember everything that needs to be asked of this patient they are seeing, which tests should be done at what intervals, when the last time the patient had that test, etc... Physicians will screw up and when they do – it's not like when Tony Romo throws an interception. That may just cause the Cowboys to lose a game. When physicians screw up, it may cost the patient a toe or a foot or their life.

So – get the most current guidelines, and if you have any trouble finding them, give me an email to donself@donself.com and let's see if we can help.

In fact, if you're looking for an EMR system, you may want to give me a call or email and I'll tell you what I know about the ones you're looking at.

Another key factor when picking an EMR system is the interconnectivity with the practice management (PM) system you currently use or are considering. Most will say they "integrate" with the PM system you're using, but when something goes wrong, you may run into the BLAME game where one says the problem is with the other software. The advantage of having one system that provides both is that you usually have a seamless transition from one to the other and one feeds into the other as well. For instance, Keith and I require that if someone wants us to put a full or moderate clinical lab in their office that they also get a Lab Interface System (LIS). We feel so strongly about this, that if they do not want to get an LIS – then we will not put a lab in. Think of how the following would work in your office, if it was set up correctly:

Mary Jones checks in at the front desk for her three month appointment and the receptionist is flagged that Mary needs a CBC, A1C, Liver Panel and glucose prior to the physician seeing her. The nurse then takes the blood, and takes Mary to the examination room.

By the time the doctor walks into the room in 5 minutes, 3 of those tests have already been run and the data is on the doctor's tablet (similar to a laptop, but lighter and easier to carry), so that when the doctor walks in – he or she has that data.

After examining Mary, the doctor may decide that he also wants a GTT and TSH, so he types that into his tablet he has in his hand and immediately, the bar coded labels are printed and someone comes in and gets the additional blood from Mary and goes back to the lab and runs the test.  Mary continues to sit in the exam room while the doctor sees another patient and as the doctor leaves that other patient, he or she sees that Mary's other lab tests are done (flags pop up on the laptop), so he stops in the room to see Mary and changes her meds and she is free to go for another 3 months and the prescriptions are sent electronically to the pharmacy. On top of that, as the labs were run, the LIS informed not only the EMR system, but also the PM, so that they were already put on the charges for the day, without anyone having to "key" them.  By the time Mary walks back up to the front, the staff knows by looking at their computer whether Mary has anything else to pay (which may be the case if Mary has Medicare and no Medigap or secondary) and when another appointment is needed.

The claim is already generated from the doctor's input on the tablet, as well as the lab system's interface, so that at the end of the day, all claims from today are batched and sent. This is a good system, in my view – and one that EVERY doctor in this country will eventually have – or at least a part of it.

It's also less expensive than paying people to keypunch codes into the computer on every visit, and those people can then be used for follow-up on claims, patient scheduling and other duties. We may not be at the Tricorder stage (Dang it Jim, I'm a doctor – not a magician) from Star Trek – but we sure are heading in that direction.

# PQRI

The 2006 Tax Relief and Health Care Act required the establishment of a Physician Quality Reporting System, including an incentive payment for eligible professionals (EPs) who satisfactorily report data on quality measures for covered professional services furnished to Medicare beneficiaries during the second half of 2007 (the 2007 reporting period). CMS named this program the Physician Quality Reporting Initiative (PQRI).

In 2007, they started with 77 quality measures that for the first time, basically told the physicians WHAT they wanted the physicians to do, why they wanted them to do it and where the guidelines originated. The bonus at that time was 1.5% of the Medicare allowed amounts for physicians that qualified, but there was no appeal or way to monitor the Medicare program (by the EPs) to make sure Medicare did give them the bonus the EPs expected.

In 2008, those 77 measures expanded to 135 measures and again to 153 measures in 2009. In November of 2009, CMS published a report when they sent out the checks to those EPs who qualified in 2008.

The report from CMS said: "More than 85,000 physicians and other eligible professionals who successfully reported quality-related data to Medicare under the 2008 Physician Quality Reporting Initiative (PQRI) received incentive payments totaling more than $92 million, the Centers for Medicare & Medicaid Services (CMS), well above the $36 million paid in 2007."

Ok—Is this the math?  $92,000,000 divided by 85,000 doctors equals $1,082.35 for the year, per provider, or $90 a month, divided by the 22.5 working days = $4 a day for the staff adding 3 CPT codes to the claims or keeping up with the registry.

Don't get me wrong as I absolutely LOVE PQRI if (big IF) the physicians actually LEARN from PQRI what it is the carriers want them to do and then actually DO it because it does result in better healthcare, better medical outcomes on the patients, reduced overall costs to the insurance companies and Medicare  and does increase the average primary care physician's net income by $100,000 a year (not the reporting - but the performance), but I find these numbers from CMS, that they are so proud of, very humorous.  $4.00 a day instead of $660 a day if the docs really used PQRI the way they should and the way we teach.

What is it going to take to get the physicians in this country to wake up and realize that PQRI will enable them to increase their income by the $660 a day if they just get off their butt and start following it?  They are looking for the "bonus" of $4.00 per day for reporting while completely ignoring the $660 a day they can make.

If you're wondering why I say that this saves the insurance carriers money, you should think about it from their perspective. We know from the NIH reports that I quoted earlier that 1 out of every 3 diabetic patients over 50 have Peripheral Arterial Disease and many of those patients will end up having a toe or a foot amputated, if the complications of the disease doesn't kill them first.

Typical amputations (when you consider the cost of the surgeon, hospital, anesthesiologist, lab, radiology, therapy and time off work) usually runs between $20,000 and $60,000 – also depending on whether it is a toe, foot or worse... Most carriers are glad to pay $120 to $140 for an ankle brachial indices to determine whether the patient has Peripheral Arterial Disease at an early enough stage so that they do not eventually have to fork over the $20,000 for an amputation. This "Evidenced Based Medicine" is a big part of not only the PQRI and AHRQ, but also the "family centered home" concept.

The 2010 PQRI currently has 175 measures and we can expect that to increase again next year. To participate in the 2010 PQRI, individual EPs may choose to report information on individual PQRI quality measures or measures groups:

> (1) to CMS on their Medicare Part B claims,
> (2) to a qualified PQRI registry, or
> (3) to CMS via a qualified electronic health record (EHR) product.

Individual EPs who meet the criteria for satisfactory submission of PQRI quality measures data via one of the reporting mechanisms above for services furnished during a 2010

PQRI reporting period will qualify to earn a PQRI incentive payment equal to 2.0% of their total estimated Medicare Part B Physician Fee Schedule (PFS) allowed charges for covered professional services furnished during that same reporting period.

If you have a practice that sees a lot of Medicare patients and they are following PQRI, that can easily equate out to a lot of money in the Reporting Bonus – on top of what the practice or clinic is making from actually FOLLOWING the guidelines of PQRI.

## PQRI IN 2015

We have tried to educate physicians on the incentives of PQRI with better medical outcomes with their patients and increased income, but the Health Reform Law signed by Obama in March 2010 calls for a different approach in 2015. Section 3002 is titled "Improvement to the Physician Quality Reporting System".

Paragraph B(8)(A)(i) describes that professionals (physicians) not satisfactorily submitting data on PQRI for covered professional services for the quality reporting period for the year will have their fee schedule reduced by 1.5%. So, not only will they (CMS) be issuing report cards on each and every EP (physicians and non physician practitioners), but they will also be fining them for not properly reporting on PQRI.

So, you will be reporting on PQRI, whether you want to or not, so it makes sense to go ahead and do due diligence now and start benefiting from the lessons you can learn in PQRI, as well as allowing your patients to benefit as well. As I've said before, the true benefit of PQRI is not your income, or saving the insurance carriers millions of dollars, it is the improved medical outcomes you will get with your patients and if that doesn't excite you – then you really are in the wrong business.

## PQRI # 1 – Diabetes: Hemoglobin A1c

The first measure of the 175 measures (you only have to report on 80% of patients that meet 3 measures) is about A1Cs on Diabetics. Medicare realizes that physicians are NOT ordering A1Cs on diabetic patients often enough and that is hurting the patients. In fact, several national carriers, such as Blue Cross, Blue Shield, Aetna and United Health Care have even sent letters to the physicians in their networks reminding them to routinely do Hemoglobin A!C tests on diabetic patients. Medicare (and other carriers) WANT doctors to order A1Cs more often.

The subtitle of this measure is: "Percentage of patients aged 18 through 75 years with diabetes mellitus who had most recent hemoglobin A1C greater than 9.0%"

"This measure is to be reported a minimum of once per reporting period for patients with diabetes mellitus seen during the reporting period. The performance period for this measure is 12 months. The most recent quality code submitted will be used for performance calculation." (This means they want you to REPORT on the A1C at least once a year, but how often you PERFORM the A1C is shown in the "Clinical Recommendation Statements") The rationale is simple: "Intensive therapy of glycosylated hemoglobin (A1c) reduces the risk of microvascular complications"

Patients with most recent hemoglobin A1c level > 9.0% This is a poor control measure. A lower rate indicates better performance (e.g., low rates of poor control indicate better care)

- 3046F: Most Recent Hemoglobin A1c  level > 9.0%
- 3046F-8P: Hemoglobin A1c not Performed
- 3044F: Most recent (HbA1c) level < 7.0%    or
- 3045F: Most recent (HbA1c) level 7.0 to 9.0%

Medicare wants patients with A1C above 7% tested on every visit to help the doctors monitor and treat. Controlled patients should be tested every 3 months, per the statements from the American Association of Clinical Endocrinologists(and those people should know a thing or two about diabetes and A1Cs).

So – how does this help the average family or Internal Medicine physician? Medicare pays an average of $13.56 for CPT 83036 and many carriers pay much more than that.

Physicians with waived testing in their office have a cost of \$8.00—with \$5.56 profit.  A physician with non-waived testing in their office has an expense ranging from \$1.00 to \$4.00 (on average) for performing A1Cs in their office.  Now – before you start thinking to yourself that you don't have the number of patients that would warrant non-waived testing in your office, you should at least take a closer look at it.

As we'll discuss later, most primary care offices seeing at least 25 patients a day should consider SOME non waived testing as the profit is much more than they actually realize.

On top of that, the best benefit is that you have the point-of-care information and that ALWAYS helps YOU to be a better doctor!

Physicians not performing this test in their office have ZERO profit since Medicare, Medciaid, Tri-care and most HMOs and PPOs prohibit pass-through billing for clinical lab tests not performed IN the physician's office.

A practice seeing 25 patients a day with 40% of the patients having diabetes sees about 10 patients a day with diabetes.  If half (5) are being seen for their quarterly visits and 10% of the other diabetics have A1Cs above 7%, that gives you 6 A1Cs a day.

If the primary care practice has the non waived lab equipment, not only does the practice get to make the 1.5% bonus from Medicare, but they also get to make $17,160 per year in profit from providing better care for the patients—based on only 6 A1Cs a day.

Now maybe $17,160 a year won't make any difference in your practice – but for many, it's a good start!

## PQRI #2: Diabetes Mellitus: (LDL-C) Control

This is another test that not only is easy to report on (PQRI Reporting), but also should be performed in most primary care offices since it gives point-of-care information, and it adds to the profit of a practice.

**Medicare wants you to report on this at least once a year.** In fact, the National Coverage Determination (NCD) that Medicare published in January 2010 states: "Any one component of the panel or a measured LDL (CPT 83721) may be reasonable and necessary **up to six times the first year** for monitoring dietary or pharmacologic therapy.

**More frequent total cholesterol HDL cholesterol, LDL cholesterol and triglyceride testing** may be indicated for marked elevations or for changes to anti-lipid therapy due to inadequate initial patient response to dietary or pharmacologic therapy. The LDL cholesterol or total cholesterol may be measured three times yearly after treatment goals have been achieved.

Ok – we know WHY they want you to run Lipid Panel, LDL and the tests and how often they want it – so how often are YOU running them on your patients that fall within the 360 or so diagnosis codes that are covered for these tests. Of course, you need to believe in the test and that it will be medically indicated and medically beneficial to the care of your patient before you run it, but we assume that you already are. If not – you may want to check with the American Association of Clinical Endocrinologists or the American College of Endocrinology as they have definitely convinced the AHRQ, PQRI, PCPI and HHS to make these guidelines the standards.

Naturally, you're wondering if you will lose money by doing these tests in your office and while we may need to perform a free diagnostic analysis) to determine whether it would be profitable for you to consider doing LDL Direct in your office, it is USUALLY profitable to be doing liver panels in your office, whether you're solo or a group primary care practice.

Again, a phone call and allowing us to ask you a few questions will let you know this answer as well.

As to the reporting so that you can qualify for the better report card when they are issued, or to get the bonus, there are 3 CPT Level II codes, depending on the LDL-C Level:

- ➤ 3048F   Most recent LDL-C <100 mg/dl
- ➤ 3049F Most recent LDL-C $\geq$ 100 mg/dl
- ➤ 3050F Most recent LDL-C $\geq$ 130 mg/dl

Now, if you haven't run an LDL-C on the patient in the previous 12 months, then you should be using 3048F-8P on the claim to show that. One reason why you may not have run the LDL-C on the patient in the previous 12 months could be due to high triglycerides.

Typically, it costs a practice about $12 to run a liver panel in the office and the usual reimbursement from Medicare is around $20, so that $8.00 adds up. Consequently, you not only get to qualify for the PQRI Reporting of 2%, but you get to make another $8.00 by following **PQRI ON EACH ONE**. How many diabetic patients do you see daily that you're letting one of the big labs make the money on that you might be missing?

You're welcome to contact the author if you want to see whether doing these in your office as non-waived might be able to get the cost down under $3.00, as we'll be glad to discuss this possibility as well, based on your patient mix, insurance mix, and many other factors that we'll ask about.

## PQRI #3 BP & Diabetes

While most doctors were very familiar with the recommended testing of the A1Cs, liver panels and LDLs on diabetic patients, many do not give the same attention to the blood pressures.

Measure 3 has a description of: "Percentage of patients aged 18 through 75 years with diabetes mellitus who had most recent blood pressure in control (less than 140/80 mmHg", although I think they are really MORE interested in the number of diabetic patients whose blood pressure is NOT in control.

Medicare is trying to get physicians to take blood pressures on diabetics on every visit (which, I believe every physician does). What they are not doing is checking for orthostatic blood pressures. The PQRI explains the rationale as "Intensive control of blood pressure in patients with diabetes reduces diabetes complications, diabetes-related deaths, strokes, heart failure, and microvascular complications."

By now, you may have heard that the American College of Cardiology reports that 61% of diabetics suffer from silent ischemia, possibly due to cardiac autonomic neuropathy. But—how do you detect it if the patient's blood pressure appears normal while sitting and the comparison of that same pressure while standing?

The PQRI says: "Blood pressure should be measured at every routine diabetes visit.

Patients found to have systolic blood pressure >130 mmHg or diastolic >80 mmHg should have blood pressure confirmed on a separate day. Orthostatic measurement of blood pressure should be performed to assess for the presence of autonomic neuropathy."

Yet—how many times a day does your staff take a patient's blood pressure while standing, after taking one while the patient was sitting or prone to see if you have a 25/10 mm mercury drop? Do you have the patient stand for at least 2 minutes prior to taking the orthostatic pressure, which is recommended since many patients will experience Delayed Orthostatic Hypotension (DOH)?

There is not a separate CPT or HCPCS code for standing blood pressure So—you're probably thinking that this is additional work and time (if you're going to make the medical assistant stand there for 2 minutes with the patient prior to actually taking the standing pressure) that you're not going to be compensated for. That is part of the office visit, but if you're also doing a Heart Rate Variability (Ansar) at the same time, you are making money as well.

First—let's look at the PQRI Pay For Reporting so that you can capture the insignificant 2% bonus by reporting on 3 different measures, while helping to ensure you get a good report card when those are eventually issued (ALL CARRIERS WILL BE USING THAT DATA).

Systolic codes (Select one CPT II code from this section):

> 3074F: Most recent systolic bp < 130 mmHg
> 3075F: Most recent systolic bp 130 - 139 mmHg
> 3077F: Most recent systolic bp greater than or equal to 140 mmHg

Diastolic codes (Select one code from this section):

> ➤ 3078F: Most recent diastolic bp less than 80 mmHg
> ➤ 3079F: Most recent diastolic bp 80 - 89 mmHg
> ➤ 3080F: Most recent diastolic bp greater than or equal to 90 mmHg

And the kicker for those who are NOT doing blood pressure checks (are you kidding me? Are there really primary care physicians NOT doing BP checks???)

Medicare says to report 2000F with an 8P modifier to indicate you have not done a BP check on the patient in the previous 12 months on the patient that is between 18 and 75 years old.

So—if you're doing the reporting—you may get $6 a day on average for the bonus—but since you have the medical necessity and the rationale for doing these—why not get much more additional clinical information on the patient, and be paid for doing it on the patients that have the medical necessity —which is what Pay For Performance is about? You've seen me talk about the Autonomic Nervous System test using Heart Rate Variability (HRV) called ANSAR. ANSAR includes a non invasive 16 minute test on the HRV specifically looking for Diabetic Autonomic Neuropathy, Cardiac Autonomic Neuropathy, Orthostatic or Postural Hypotension and more.

Medicare's average allowed amount is more than $148 and Medicare's LCD on it includes diabetes, hypertension, CHF, COPD and sleep difficulties in every state except 1 (California).

As an example, on one Friday in December, I trained a 4 provider practice in Arkansas on how to do the test and the benefits of the test and on Monday, they scheduled 30 patients that needed it.   They diagnosed, just on Monday—several patients with cardiac autonomic neuropathy, several more with orthostatic hypotension and changed the meds on 2 patients that were receiving too many Beta-blockers that had greatly diminished the quality of life the patients had been experiencing for months.

Medicare and the private carriers want you doing PQRI because it saves lives and improves lives.  It saves the payers money because the problems are caught earlier—when they can be treated—instead of when it requires catastrophic care.   Isn't that what good medicine is really about?

# PQRI # 51 – (COPD): Spirometry Evaluation

The description of Measure 51 says "Percentage of patients aged 18 years and older with a diagnosis of COPD who had spirometry evaluation results documented"

The rationale behind requesting this data on COPD patients is pretty simple.  "Evaluation of lung function for a patient with COPD is vital to determine what treatments are needed and whether those treatments are effective."  The sad part is that most primary care physicians are not screening for COPD, so by the time they diagnose that there is a problem, the patient already has COPD.

You screen for hypertension by doing blood pressure checks on patients on every visit, probably because cardiac disease is the number 1 killer. We screen for diabetes by running A1Cs and glucose tests. Yet— we're not routinely screening for the number 4 killer, COPD, and (partly) because of this, we're expecting COPD to be the number 3 killer in our country by 2020 (per the National Institute of Health).

The clinical Recommendations included in the PQRI (from the American Thoracic Society) state: "Spirometry should be performed in all patients suspected of COPD. This is necessary for diagnosis, assessment of severity of the disease and for following the progress of the disease."

For the diagnosis and assessment of COPD, spirometry is the gold standard as it is the most reproducible, standardized, and objective way of measuring airflow limitation. FEV1/FVC < 70% and a post-bronchodilator FEV1 < 80% predicted confirms the presence of airflow limitation that is not fully reversible, per the National Heart Lung and Blood Institute.

OK—so they want us to test those SUSPECTED of having COPD to determine if they have it and then they want tests to see what treatment is most effective. If we report that—they're willing to give the doctor a 2% bonus for the Pay For Reporting.

Oh yeah—if we do that we also get paid for Performing the test (Pay For Performance).

Let's discuss the Pay For Reporting first, so we can qualify for the $6 a day bonus checks.

First, we're required to have a diagnosis code for COPD on the claim, which includes 491.0, 491.1, 491.20, 491.21, 491.22, 491.8, 491.9, 492.0, 492.8, or 496 and the CPT code 99201, 99202, 99203, 99204, 99205, 99212, 99213, 99214, 99215 must be charged on the claim.

Then, we're supposed to report on at least 3 measures (so far, we've discussed 1, 2, 3 and now 51) and at least 80% of our patients falling within those measures, to qualify for the 1.5%.

To report, you need CPT II code:

3023F: Spirometry results documented & reviewed

Or if the results were not documented, append a modifier (1P, 2P, or 3P) to code 3023F to report why.

> 1P: Documentation of medical reason(s) for not documenting and reviewing spirometry results
> 2P: Documentation of patient reason(s) for not documenting and reviewing spirometry results
> 3P: Documentation of system reason(s) for not documenting and reviewing spirometry results
> 8P: Spirometry results not documented and reviewed, reason not otherwise specified

This one is so easy that Al Gore could do this math. If you do a spirometry (94010), you make $28.90 (avg) from Medicare. If you do a pre and a post bronchodilator exam, you bill out 94060 and you just made $54 from Medicare and the patient. If you're using a spirometer to perform either of these, you have just checked the mechanics of the lung to see if there is an FEV1/FVC less than 70%.

Yet—if the mechanics of the lung are ok—you still don't know anything about the diffusion, gas exchange, etc... because you did not check the diffusion or gas exchange when you did only a spirometry or a pre-post spirometry.

You have a choice. Do you make the $54.56 from Medicare or do you perform a real PFT in your office whereby you get very useful information including the vital capacity, maximum breathing capacity, functional residual capacity, thoracic gas volume, determination of resistance to airflow, evaluation of aerosol or nebulizer and carbon monoxide diffusing capacity?

The PFT devices that do all of this costs about $47,000, which on a 5 year lease runs about $1050 per month (based on good credit with a $1.00 buyout and no payments for the first 3 months). If you only did 2 tests per day, your gross income would be about $11,000.

That gives you a monthly net of about $10,000—which isn't going to make you rich. That's only about $120,000 a year net or $600,000 profit over the 5 year lease. If this interests you, you may want to call the author and discuss it to see if you have the right patient and insurance mix to consider adding it to your practice.

If you're wondering who in your office can do the test, Florida is the only state that requires a licensed respiratory technician perform it—to the best of my knowledge, although that may change (which is why I always check the current NCDs and LCDs immediately prior to recommending spirometry or PFT to any physician.

In fact, Florida requires the licensed respiratory technician or the physician personally perform the spirometry and my estimation is that 80% of the physicians I've talked to in Florida doing spirometers are not meeting that Medicare guideline. The respiratory tech is not an RN, LVN, MA, either. Pay for Reporting gives you about $6 a day. Pay For\ Performance helps you detect, diagnose and treat those patients that are non diagnostic on the mechanics but have severe problems and it gives you about $400 a day profit, plus the $6. PQRI can be your friend if you learn from it.

## PQRI #126 – Diabetes And Foot Exams

*"Foot ulceration is the most common single precursor to lower extremity amputations among persons with diabetes*. Treatment of infected foot wounds accounts for up to one-quarter of all inpatient hospital admissions for people with diabetes in the United States.

Peripheral sensory neuropathy in the absence of perceived trauma is the primary factor leading to diabetic foot ulcerations. *Approximately 45-60% of all diabetic ulcerations are purely neuropathic*. In people with diabetes, 22.8% have foot problems – such as amputations and numbness – compared with 10% of non-diabetics.

*Over the age of 40 years old, 30% of people with diabetes have loss of sensation in their feet* (Diabetes with Peripheral Circulatory Disorders)." This is a quote from the PQRI Measure #126.

This is additional justification for physicians to be checking for Peripheral Arterial Disease. Measure 126 allows clinicians to report on PQRI for the examination they should be performing quarterly to annually (depending on the symptoms present) on their patients. I imagine this is perfect for the Podiatrists to qualify for PQRI so that they can get the bonus—but the key point here is that it leads us to believe that some physicians are NOT taking diabetic peripheral neuropathy serious enough.

If 30% of the diabetics in this country, over 40, have a loss of sensation in their feet—then primary care physicians should be testing these people for Peripheral Arterial Disease much more often than they have been. Accordingly, the referral of patients to Podiatrists by primary care physicians should be at an all time high so as to help the patients prevent the amputations.

These numbers also indicate that the number of ANSAR tests should be increased dramatically—since that detects the Diabetic Autonomic Neuropathy at an early enough stage that proactive treatment can begin. It also helps the clinician treat the DAN before it becomes Peripheral or Cardiac Autonomic Neuropathy.

A discussion I had last week with a Neurologist in Oklahoma confirmed that patients with Peripheral Neuropathy definitely have Autonomic Neuropathy PRIOR to the peripheral!

# New & Established Patients

There is as much confusion about when you can charge a new patient visit as there is about whether President Obama was born in Hawaii or Kenya. CMS defines a new patient as a patient who has not received any professional services, i.e., evaluation and management service or other face-to-face service (e.g., surgical procedure) from the physician or physician group practice (same physician specialty) within the previous three years.

For example, if a professional component of a previous procedure is billed in a 3-year time-period, e.g., a lab interpretation is billed and no E/M service or other face-to-face service with the patient is performed, then this patient remains a new patient for the initial visit. An interpretation of a diagnostic test, reading an x-ray or EKG etc., in the absence of an E/M service or other face-to-face service with the patient does not affect the designation of a new patient.

Where this gets confusing is when a physician in a group practice of Family Physicians (specialty code 08) sees a patient for the first time, and that patient has been seen at the hospital the week before by another physician in that group. In that case, it would not be a new patient. It doesn't matter if the clinic needs to create a new patient chart or not. That patient would NOT be considered to be new by Medicare, Medicaid and just about every carrier I've ever heard of, since it has been within 3 years since seen.

Conversely, if the physician that saw the patient in the hospital was an Internist (specialty code 11 with Medicare), and the physician seeing the patient in the office (not following up what the other physician did) was a Family physician, legally you could charge a new patient visit, as the specialty makes the difference. I'm not saying you SHOULD bill a new patient, but I am saying that Medicare allows it.

Occasionally, the question arises about a physician who saw a patient two years ago in one practice and since then, the physician has moved to your practice and the patient is seen in your practice by a physician of the same specialty. Technically, this would be a new patient, unless the physician that saw the patient 2 years ago was the patient to see them today, in which case it would be an established patient, but again, whether you should charge them for a new patient visit or not is a call you should make.

We do not want to adversely affect the attempts we are making in getting new patients by doing something that is legal, yet perhaps is not viewed as being appropriate by the patient (and some staff members). This may be one of those instances where just because you CAN, that doesn't mean you SHOULD.

# Medicare Advanced Beneficiary Notice (ABN)

The use of the ABN is required by Medicare to alert patients when a service will not be paid by Medicare and to allow the patient to choose to pay for the service or to refuse the service. If the patient is going to sign the ABN, they must do so BEFORE the service is rendered, or the ABN becomes invalid.

If we do not have a signed ABN from the patient and Medicare denies the service, we have to write off the charge and cannot request the patient to pay for it. The only exception is for statutorily excluded services (those that Medicare never covers like cosmetic surgery and complete physicals for example). In this case, we can still bill the patient for the non-covered service regardless of having a signed ABN.

In fact, when you have the patient sign the ABN, the Medicare allowed is no longer a factor and you can charge the Medicare patient your usual non Medicare charge for the service and you can collect from the patient at the time of service. Medicare and the Centers for Medicare & Medicaid Services (CMS) do not prohibit you from collecting at the time of service.

It is, however, a good idea to have the ABN signed for non-covered services so the patient still is aware that they are responsible and we have proof that they knew. Typically, the patient will call our office when they receive our bill and state that "they were never told", "they weren't aware", or a similar complaint.

With a signed ABN, we have proof that we have their informed consent to provide the service and their agreement to be financially responsible for the service. In the past, Medicare had a "Notice of Exclusion of Medicare Benefits" (NEMB) that we could provide to the patient (no signature required) to alert them of Medicare's non-covered services. The ABN has replaced the NEMB.

The typical reasons that Medicare will not cover certain services and that would be applicable to most offices are:

1. Statutorily Excluded service/procedure (non-covered service)
2. Frequency Limitations
3. Not Medically Necessary

**Statutorily Excluded** items are services that Medicare will never cover, such as (not a complete list):

- Complete physicals (excluding Welcome to Medicare Screenings, with caveats)
- Most immunizations (Hepatitis A, Td)
- DME supplies (splints, personal comfort items)
- Cosmetic surgery

For these items, it is a good idea (not a requirement) to complete the ABN and have the patient check the appropriate box under options and sign the ABN. For the sake of any billing department, I strongly encourage the use of ABN's for statutorily excluded items.

**Frequency Limitations** are for services that have a specific time frame between services. For example, for normal pap smears Medicare allows one every 24 months. If the patient wants one every 12 months for their piece of mind, Medicare will pay for year one and the patient will pay for year two and that pattern continues. The ABN needs to be on file for the year that the patient is responsible for paying. If the patient fits Medicare's guidelines for "high risk" they are allowed to have the pap every 12 months and no ABN is required.

Services that are not considered **Medically Necessary** are those that do not have a covered diagnosis code based on Local Coverage Determinations. One example is for excision of a lesion. If the lesion is being removed because the patient just doesn't like how it looks, that is considered cosmetic surgery. If the lesion is showing some changes (i.e. bleeding, growing, changing color, etc), then it is considered medically necessary because it potentially can be malignant. The removal needs to have diagnosis coding to substantiate the medical necessity and Medicare has Local Coverage Determinations that lists all the codes/coding combinations that Medicare will approve for payment.

A rule of thumb in trying to discern the necessity of ABN's is to discern whether or not Medicare ever will cover the service and if there may be some times that the service isn't covered. The times the service isn't covered, an ABN is required.

To illustrate this point, I will use two examples:

➢ *EKG's are covered for certain cardiac and respiratory conditions. The only time an EKG is covered for preventive screening is during the patient's first year enrolled in the Medicare program and when being doing during the Welcome to Medicare screening. After that time, Medicare will never cover an EKG for preventive screening.*
*To notify the patient of this and to show that the patient agrees to be financially responsible for the EKG, an ABN will need to be completed.*

➢ *Another example is for the Tetanus immunization. Medicare will cover tetanus when medically necessary; basically if the patient has cut themselves and the tetanus is provided due to that injury. If the tetanus is provided to the patient because it has been ten years since the last tetanus and the tetanus is not in response to a recent injury, then it will be non-covered because it is not "medically necessary" and the ABN will need to be on file.*

You should not leave any blanks in the ABN, or it may be deemed invalid.  The "Options" box can only be completed by the patient and it states that "We cannot choose a box for you", as that would appear to be coercion.  A "blanket" ABN, (one that is signed by the patient for all services provided within a certain time period) is not acceptable and is illegal.

In addition, there is a small area to provide additional information that can be used by either the patient or the provider's office. This could be anything pertinent to the information that the ABN covers. The bottom of the form is where the patient signs and dates.

We keep the original ABN in the chart behind the progress note for that day. We **MUST** provide a copy of the signed ABN to the patient.

The current ABN form with instructions can be found at:

www.cms.hhs.gov/BNI/Downloads/ABNFormInstructions.zip

If a procedure is denied by Medicare and the physician does not have a signed ABN prior to the service being rendered, the service cannot be billed to the patient and will need to be written off the physician's books. Sometimes a patient may refuse to sign the ABN, and in this situation, it is appropriate for the physician to document the refusal and sign, along with having a witness sign. Medicare will accept this and the patient can be billed for the service if denied by Medicare. My thoughts are simple.

WHY perform the service when the patient refuses to sign the ABN acknowledging they will pay for it. If they refuse – then they are saying they won't pay for it – so if you provide it – you will be doing so for free – unless you have some way of magically teleporting the money from the patient's wallet into your hand without the patient's knowledge.

It seems ludicrous, in most instances, for you to go ahead and perform the service and then expect the patient to pay, but there will be some physicians who will go ahead and render the service – knowing the patient refuses to pay – and then in a Pollyanna fashion, tell the staff to bill the patient.

There are some additional billing requirements in the form of modifiers. The modifiers are applied to the service that the ABN was utilized:

**GA**: The ABN is signed, but the service may not be covered.

**GY**: A "statutorily excluded" service.

**GZ**: The service is expected to be denied as not reasonable or necessary. This is typically used when there is a secondary payer that requires the Medicare denial before they pay benefits.

The use of the ABN is often misunderstood; however, it is the only way a patient can be informed about their financial responsibility prior to agreeing to a service being rendered. This is an issue that the OIG has reportedly been interested in investigating for fraud and abuse, and one that we can expect the Recovery Audit Contractors to center in on.

Note: Much of the content in the ABN area was written by Charlene Burgett, M.S.-HCM, CPC, CMA, CPM, CCP, CMCS, who is also a friend and manages a group practice in Arizona.

# Using A Nurse Practitioner Or Physician Assistant

I've received treatment from physicians who had the bedside manner of Gregory House and I've had physicians who had a great patient relationship. Similarly, it has been my experience to deal with some physicians whose history and examination were exemplary (I'm thinking right now about Kevin Riccitelli D.O. in Lawton, Oklahoma that probably gave my wife the best office visit that I've seen and Jim Holleman D.O. in Tyler, Texas who did the same for my father) and some who would probably have missed a 2 inch lesion on my forehead for being so much in a hurry that they did a terrible job.

Too often, I find the primary care physicians burdened down with the simple colds, lesions, earaches, stiff joints, etc... and they are not able to do the kind of care on their chronically ill patients that they want to and that the patients need.   When I find this, it's generally been my experience that the physician needs a Non Physician Practitioner (NPP) to help them and it is almost ALWAYS able to improve the medical care of the patients and very profitable for the practice.

Recently, someone emailed me some median numbers for the pay of Nurse Practitioners in 2009.  It listed the median pay in the country for all NPs combined at about $82,000.  For Family Practice (without Obstetrics), it was about $78,000.  For Internal Medicine it was closer to $82,000.  The report did not break out the compensation by geographical regions.

I've seen them working for as low as $39 an hour and in some places, the going rate seems to be closer to $68 an hour.

Regardless of what you're paying a GOOD Nurse Practitioner or Physician Assistant, in most primary care offices, they'll generate $235 an hour collectable. Compare that to the $45 to $70 an hour they cost, and you're making a good profit – WHILE making sure that every patient has enough face-to-face time with a provider that they are receiving good medical care.

The last time you went to see a primary care provider, did you feel like you had an ample amount of face-to-face time with that provider to cover your problems, questions and when you left, did you feel that you were well taken care of? You want your own patients to feel that way, hopefully.

## Incident-To Billing

Medicare is the only carrier that we've seen it written in stone as to how you can and cannot bill for the services of a Non Physician Practitioner.

It is best to bill under incident-to (under the physician's number), when it is appropriate and legal, since the claim will be submitted under the physician's name that is not only supervising the service, but is also on the premises (in the suite) when the service is rendered.

In this case, the Medicare allowed amount is identical to the amount it would be if the service was provided by the physician and the Medicare claim is no different than if the physician did the service.

Every Non Physician Practitioner should have a Medicare number, as there will always be times when you will have to bill under the NPP's number (called direct billing) and there may be times when you can bill under incident-to (under the physician's number).

The rule for direct billing for Non Physician Practitioners are found in the Medicare Internet Only Manual 100-02, 15, 190 with some additional billing stuff in IOM 100-04, 12, 110.
In my 25 years of medical billing experience, one of the most knowledgeable consultants helping providers stay compliant in the areas of incident-to billing is Quinten (Quin) Buechner, CPC in Cumberland, Wisconsin.

In IOM 100-02, 15, 190 the rules say:
The services of a PA may be covered under Part B, if all of the following requirements are met:

- They are the types that are considered physician's services if furnished by a doctor of medicine or osteopathy (MD/DO);
- They are performed by a person, who meets all the PA qualifications,

- They are performed under the general supervision of an MD/DO;
- The PA is legally authorized to perform the services in the state in which they are performed; and
- They are not otherwise precluded from coverage because of one of the statutory exclusions.

**(WHEN NOT BILLING INCIDENT-TO, THERE IS NOTHING RESTRICTING NPP SERVICES TO EITHER NEW OR ESTABLISHED PATIENTS).**

If covered PA services are furnished, services and supplies furnished incident to the PA's services may also be covered if they would have been covered when furnished incident to the services of an MD/DO.

Examples of the types of services that NPPs may provide include services that traditionally have been reserved to physicians, such as physical examinations (DOES NOT RESTRICT TO ONLY ESTABLISHED PATIENTS), minor surgery, setting casts for simple fractures, interpreting x-rays, and other activities that involve an independent evaluation or treatment of the patient's condition.

In IOM 100-04,12,110.3.C the IOM says "A PA like a NP may bill using their own provider number. All claims for NPP services must be made on an assignment basis."

The easy way to remember when you can bill incident-to

or when you must bill direct, is the 3 **NP** rule. If you are considering billing for a mid level provider, consider:

1. If there is **No Physician** in the suite, you have to bill under the Non Physician Practitioner's number.

2. If it is a **New Problem**, you have to bill under the Non Physician Practitioner's number.

3. If it is a **New Patient**, you have to bill under the Non Physician Practitioner's number.

Many times, if you give the patients a choice when they call for an appointment (it will be 2 weeks before Dr. Kildare can see you, but our Nurse Practitioner can see you this Wednesday if you prefer), you may find that patients select the option of seeing the NPP.

A common misconception with billing personnel (and some Non Physician Practitioners) is that a Nurse Practitioner or Physician Assistant can only bill a level 1, 2 or 3 visit. That is about as untrue as a liberal saying they will not raise taxes.

A Non Physician Practitioner can bill any level of service as a physician can bill, as long as it is medically necessary, they are doing the work and they are documenting it properly.

The number of times that an NPP is under-coded by

either their own ignorance or the ignorance of an improperly educated billing staff is almost criminal.

Not keeping the billing personnel up to date on changes is tantamount to putting handcuffs on the front desk so that they cannot hold their hand out to collect cash. It is utter stupidity for a physician to NOT pay for their staff to attend well taught seminars and conventions on coding changes. In fact, it makes about as much sense to educate them as it does for physicians to have to be updated on changes in medicine. Yet – I see physicians spending $300 a night on luxurious hotels, $125 for dinner for two for them and their spouse, $150 greens fees and more to be updated on CMEs a the conventions I speak at, while moaning and whining about spending $100 for their staff to attend a coding and billing convention. Good business is making sure that your staff is up to date, as they may be the only thing keeping you from taking showers with guys named Bubba in prison or picking up trash on the side of the highway in an orange jumpsuit!

## Incident-To Is Not For Physicians

If you add a physician to your practice, you CANNOT bill incident-to for another physician's services. Yes, you can bill incident-to for mid levels who work for you or the RN or MA or anyone else—under incident-to—but NOT another physician.

CMS has said that physician's do NOT meet the definition of support or ancillary personnel and therefore cannot have their services billed under the number of another physician.

Billing under another physician's name (as in incident-to) is specifically stated as being wrong in the Medicare Program Integrity Manual, (IOM 100-08 Ch4: www.cms.hhs.gov/Manuals/IOM/list.asp#TopOfPage . In the law, there are cases where billing one physician under another physician's numbers constitutes fraudulent representation. We do not recommend this for Medicare or for non Medicare since it seems to be a violation of every PPO and Insurance contract we have reviewed so far. If you are adding another physician to your practice, you should make sure you give yourself plenty of time prior to their start to get them credentialed. It is almost never a problem getting Medicare to issue a retroactive number, dating back to the date (within 30 days) they start seeing Medicare patients, but it is best to get their credentialing started as soon as you are sure they are coming to your practice. Some private and PPO carriers have been known to take six months to get it done.

## Billing Family Members

This question arises, usually with Medicare rules, but there are some that believe that a physician can NEVER give away services for free and others believe that the practice cannot bill employees or any family members. Both rules of thought are incorrect, and we'll discuss both.

President Clinton tried to take over 100% control of healthcare back in the early 90s and he and his wife were unsuccessful, so they didn't stop you from giving away free services. President Obama is trying to do the same thing 17 years later and he hasn't accomplished this YET, so you still control your practice.

You can give away any service for free that you wish to, in spite of the fear of Big Brother applying Stark laws to you that are not applicable if you want to give away a service to your pastor or neighbor or military personnel or whomever YOU want to give it away to.

Yes – there is a law and regulation that says you cannot give away something for free if it will be an incentive for that person to refer patients to you, or something equally non applicable for 99% of the times that physicians wish to give away services.

Naturally, if you ask your attorney about this, they will warn you that you shouldn't ever give something away for free as SOMEONE may think that it was an incentive, but it is their job to protect your buttocks. It doesn't matter if the possibilities that it could cause you problems are so remote that Mr. Spock on the Enterprise couldn't calculate the odds.

Regarding the rules in billing the physician's family members, Medicare has specific rules regulating who you cannot bill the Medicare program for.

Medicare regulations do not provide payment under Part A or Part B of Medicare for expenses that constitute charges by immediate relatives of the beneficiary or by members of his/her household. The intent of this exclusion is to bar Medicare payment for items and services furnished by physicians or suppliers who would ordinarily be furnished gratuitously because of the relationship of the beneficiary to the person imposing the charge.

This exclusion applies to items and services rendered by a related physician or supplier, even if the bill or claim is submitted by an unrelated individual or by a partnership or professional corporation.

It applies to items and services furnished incident to a physician's professional services (e.g., by the physician's nurse or technician) only if the physician who ordered or supervised the services has an excluded relationship to the beneficiary.

## Immediate Relative

The following degrees of relationship are included within the definition of immediate relative:

- husband and wife
- natural or adoptive parent, child and sibling
- stepparent, stepchild, stepbrother and stepsister
- father-in-law, mother-in-law, son-in-law, daughter-in-law, brother-in-law and sister-in-law
- grandparent and grandchild
- spouse of grandparent or grandchild

A brother-in-law or sister-in-law relationship does not exist between a physician (or supplier) and his/her spouse's brother-in-law or sister-in law.

A father-in-law or mother-in-law relationship does not exist between a physician and his/her spouse's stepfather or stepmother.

A step-relationship and an in-law relationship continue to exist even if the marriage upon which the relationship is based terminates through divorce or through the death of one of the parties.

For example, if a physician treats his stepfather after the death of his natural mother the service is considered furnished to an immediate relative and is excluded from coverage. Another example is if a physician treats his stepfather after the stepfather and natural mother are divorced, the service is considered furnished to an immediate relative and is excluded from coverage. Finally, if a physician treats his father-in-law after the death of his wife, the service is considered furnished to an immediate relative and is excluded from coverage.

## Members of Patient's Household

Also excluded are people sharing a common abode with the patient as a part of a single family unit, including those related by blood, marriage, or adoption, domestic employees and others who live together as part of a single family unit. A mere roomer or boarder is not included.

# Charges for Physician and Physician-Related Services

This exclusion applies if the physician has an excluded relationship to the beneficiary. It includes services that are furnished, ordered, supervised or services that are incident to his/her services (e.g., by the physician's nurse or technician). It also includes services of a physician who belongs to a professional corporation.

The term "professional corporation" means a corporation that is completely owned by one or more physicians or is owned by other health care professionals as authorized by State law.

It is operated for the purpose of conducting the practice of medicine, osteopathy, dentistry, podiatry, optometry or chiropractic. Any physician or group of physicians that is incorporated constitutes a professional corporation. (Generally, physicians who are incorporated identify themselves by adding letters such as P.C. or P.A. after their title.)

# Charges for Items Furnished by Non-Physician Suppliers

This exclusion applies to charges imposed by a non-physician supplier that is not incorporated, whether the supplier is owned by a sole proprietor who is related to the patient or by a partnership in which even one of the partners is related to the patient. The exclusion does not apply to charges imposed by a corporation (other than a professional corporation), regardless of the patient's relationship to any of the stockholders, officers or directors of the corporation or to the person who furnished the service.

# CODING

## Consultations

Not all physicians and not all clinics have been following the rules regarding new patient office visits and consultations. It has actually shocked me to see how many surgical and other specialists have classified every new patient as a consultation – even though there was no opinion being requested. On quite a few occasions, I've told these same people that they needed to stop using consultations when the patient was not actually sent there for a consultation, but that a new patient visit code was appropriate. It was the same reaction as if I told them that Bill Clinton had been nominated by Focus on the Family as the Moral Man of the Year for 1996. They were shocked.

A consultation is a request for an opinion from one health care provider to another, requiring a face-to-face with the patient (not 2 doctors stopping in the hospital hallway discussing a patient). A consultation requires all three components of documentation that I covered earlier (history, exam and medical decision making) and as equally important – someone REQUESTING the consultation.

As a patient, I have seen the staff ask me on a new patient visit to a specialist who my primary care physician is and when I checked out, noticed that I had been billed as a consultation – when it was I who looked up the specialist in the phone book and made the appointment on my own initiative.

That was not a consultation and it did prompt a discussion with the office manager and what I refer to as a "Come To Jesus" talk. (A Come To Jesus talk is a serious talk about the very serious consequences of not doing what you need to do) At first, the office manager was offended that a patient would presume to know more than she did about medical office coding until I explained that a call would be forthcoming to the insurance carrier that I was a policyholder of and that they were contracted with which would disclose exactly what fraud is. I also explained that a similar call to Medicare would be taking place since I knew that most physicians and offices code their non Medicare patients identical (in most aspects) to the Medicare patients. The fact that the physician was also a previous client and happened to walk into hearing range of the conversation and interjected himself made the final difference. He knew that I would not put up with insurance or Medicare fraud and he was unaware of it to that point and assured me that they would change their ways.

So – a consult is one provider asking another for advice and the fact that the consulting physician initiates treatment either at the consult or subsequent to the consult does not negate the fact that first visit can be a consultation and be billed as a consultation. But, if the patient heard about your doctor from a friend or a television ad or found you in the phonebook or on the internet – that is NOT a consultation by any stretch of the imagination.

If the family physician sends you to a gastroenterologist to take care of a bleeding ulcer, that FP is not asking for an opinion. He or she is sending you to someone else to take care of the problem and that first visit in the office is a new patient office visit and not a consultation. To charge it as such should be treated as insurance fraud, in my opinion. That gastroenterologist is not going to render their opinion.

They are going to take care of the bleeding ulcer and they'll probably copy the Family physician as simple professional courtesy and to think otherwise is definitely delving into the gray area too much. Keep your coding and billing in the white area and stay out of the gray and black area as it is not worth it to get too close to fraud and abuse.

A consultation can be on a new or an established patient as they are not specific to either in the CPT codebook. In fact, back when Medicare paid for them, they also did not limit consultation codes to new or established patients.

2010 is now here, and it is not just a video at Blockbuster. As it pertains to coding and billing, a huge issue has raised its head in 2010. Medicare announced it will no longer pay for consultation codes in 2010. Why? Mostly it is due to the misuse of this service. Medicare paid more than $4 Billion for consultations. The OIG found that more than $1.1 Billion was paid incorrectly. This decision has panicked some coders and physicians, resulting in rumors, bad information and innovative suggestions on how to bypass claims edits, which is never a good idea.

As I said earlier, many physicians abused consultations and billed consultation codes when they shouldn't have. On the other hand, many primary care physicians who were rendering their opinion to surgeons on pre-operative visits were NOT billing consultations when they should. Medicare tried for years to educate physicians and many refused to use consultation codes appropriately – so like a parent whose child refuses to take proper care of their toy may either ground the child or take it away, Medicare discontinued payment for them as of January 1st, 2010.

They did NOT classify them as non covered (which would be dangerous to do – knowing that some physicians would then bill the patient directly for the non covered service). The classified them as status I (as in the word "invalid"), which is "Not valid for Medicare purposes. Medicare uses another code for reporting of, and payment for, these services".

This has caused as much confusion to coders, billers, managers and physicians as the Electoral College caused Al Gore in 2000. If you don't understand the basics of it, you will never understand the complexity of it. The basics of it is simple. Medicare stopped paying for them so act as if the codes do not exist.

## Consultation Crosswalk

Unfortunately, even though the consult deletion is simple, there will always be people that will try to make it complicated and those are the people asking and demanding a crosswalk. These are generally people who want others to spell it out for them instead of them having to learn how to code the visit. I'll try to keep it simple for you, with some bullet points:

- There used to be 5 outpatient consult codes (99241-99245).
- There used to be 5 inpatient consult codes (99251 – 99255).
- All consultations required all 3 documentation components (history, exam, mdm)
- There are 5 new patient office visit codes (99201 – 99205) which require all 3 (history, exam, mdm).
- There are 5 established office/outpatient visit codes (99211 – 92215) which require ANY 2 of the 3 (history, exam, mdm)

- There are 3 initial inpatient care codes (99221 – 99223) that require all 3 (history, exam, mdm)
- There are 3 subsequent inpatient codes (99231 – 99233) that require ANY 2 of 3 (history, exam, mdm)
- There is no crosswalk for billing purposes.
- You now have to use your coding skills by looking at the documentation to select the level of Hx,Exam and MDM for the appropriate coding area.

Now, you will see a crosswalk issued by someone, but you will not see it on www.donself.com as that is not something that I want you using. It was not designed for billing purposes, but it was designed strictly for RVU purposes. It will not work for billing purposes, but if someone were to give it to an unsuspecting soul, they may try to use it for billing purposes and get into trouble. The reason I do not put it on donself.com is the same reason you do not give a teenage boy a condom and tell him to not have sex until he is married. Your words said one thing, but your actions said something else.

You wouldn't give your 10 year old a pack of cigarettes and lighter to carry around and tell them that they shouldn't smoke, so why give your doctor a crosswalk that will harm them?

CMS has published information and provided webinars in order to dispel rumors, provide more accurate answers, to reduce administrative costs from incorrectly coded and billed claims, prevent fraud and abuse, to ensure continuity of revenue to providers, and to ensure providers, coders, and biller stay in line with compliance requirements for coding and billing of services to Medicare members.

In MM6740, Medicare provides the following information as it pertains to providers providing inpatient services.

Conventional medical practice is that physicians making a referral and physicians accepting a referral would document the request to provide an evaluation for the patient. In order to promote proper coordination of care, these physicians should continue to follow appropriate medical documentation standards and communicate the results of an evaluation to the requesting physician. This is not to be confused with the specific documentation requirements that previously applied to the use of the consultation codes.

In the inpatient hospital setting and nursing facility setting, any physicians and qualified NPPs who perform an initial evaluation may bill an initial hospital care visit code (CPT code 99221 – 99223) or nursing facility care visit code (CPT 99304 – 99306), where appropriate.

> ➤ In all cases, physicians will bill the available code that most appropriately describes the level of the services provided.

Medicare says that in situations where you have Commercial Primary (which could pay for consults) and Medicare Secondary (which no longer pays), you have two choices:

1. Bill the consult to the primary. Once the primary pays, you bill Medicare with the appropriate E/M for the visit such as 99201-99215 as an example), you accompany the claim with the primary eob and the claim shows the primary payment or
2.
3. Simply bill the primary and Medicare the appropriate E/M code altogether.

## Medicare Secondary In Hospital

My advice is a bit different:

1. If Medicare primary – bill visit codes, making sure you use AI if you're the admitting physician

2. If other than Medicare – continue using consultation codes as you've done in the past

3. If Medicare is secondary, and consult is in the office – bill consult codes on primary as you'll make lots more money than office visit codes.

4. If Medicare is secondary and consult is in the hospital – on the first time you see the pt in the hospital – bill 99221-99223 and you make more than if you did a consult code and you don't have to change the code on secondary claim.

5. If Medicare is secondary and consult is in the hospital – on a subsequent visit – use the consult code on primary and it doesn't matter if you bill Medicare secondary as you're still making more money than if you did subsequent codes.

## Pre-Op Physicals Are Consultations

I recommend that the primary care physicians performing a pre-operative physical do several things:

- Learn to say no to the surgeons when asked to do a pre-op when the patient does NOT have a chronic disease complicating surgery.
- Ask the surgeon for the symptom, diagnosis or systemic condition that warrants the pre-op be performed by someone other than the surgeon.
- Use the diagnosis that prompts the need for them to do the pre-op instead of the surgeon doing the pre-op.

I'm trying to anticipate the future when the insurers figure out they are paying twice for the same thing and then they will want money back from one of the two docs as someone should not have been paid.

OK – we know that when a surgeon gets paid for replacing a funny bone in a patient, the amount they are paid includes normal pre-op, surgery and routine post-op.

The doctor doing the surgery is a doctor. He or she went to medical school and learned that the funny bone is connected to the arm bone which is connected to the shoulder bone which is connected... ok – you get the point. They are allegedly proficient enough that the patient is going to entrust their life to the person in hopes the surgeon doesn't show up drunk, stoned, pre-occupied, etc... hoping that they'll do a good job. So – the carrier is paying this fee to the surgeon.

So – why is another doctor needed to do a pre-op? Is the surgeon not qualified or are they incompetent? Why should the insurance carrier pay twice for the normal pre-op? Why should they pay the surgeon and a primary care doctor? What is the medical necessity for a second doctor to be involved? If there is no chronic disease, systemic condition or problem other than the reason for the surgery – why can't the surgeon do the normal pre-op that they're being paid to do?

Is it because the surgeon wants someone else to share the blame if they screw up? Is it that the surgeon doesn't want to be bothered to do the pre-operative workup that the hospitals and anesthesiologists expect?

What is going to happen when the insurance carriers, including Medicare, figure this out and they come back to get money back from someone? Who are they going to get it from?

The surgeon didn't use the appropriate 54 and 55 modifier and the primary care doctor hasn't been taught to use the surgery code with a 56 modifier (which they should be taught this by their coders).

My thought is that if we do not give the diagnosis code that supports the REASON the primary care doc is needed, who will the carriers come back to when they want to recoup money?

# Office & Other Outpatient Visit Codes

Now, the nurse or MA or whomever has taken the patient back to the exam room and the physician has listened to the patients complaints, obtained a history (remember – it must be the physician or mid level that documents the history of present illness), examined the patient and made a determination of care and documented the visit. The level of documentation and the medical necessity supporting that level of documentation is evident, so the provider is now trying to determine which level of service should be billed. With a new patient, you have the CPT codes (issued by the AMA) 99201 through 99215 to choose from. With a new patient visit, you must have documented all 3 basic components (history, exam and medical decision making). If the physician performed any procedures during the encounter, you can and should bill for those, in addition to the office visit, as long as the visit was significant and separately identifiable.

In other words, if the procedure and it's related examination is removed from the progress note, is there still a clear medical necessity for the visit and is the level of history, exam and medical decision making substantial enough to support the level of visit billed? If so – you bill the visit with a 25 modifier, so that the visit is not bundled into the procedure.

If the level of visit (history, exam and medical decision making) is not significant enough to warrant a visit in addition to the procedure, then a visit should not be billed. You should not automatically assign a modifier 25 to every visit just to get it paid or that is fraudulent billing. You should only bill the visit with a 25 modifier when it meets the requirements of being separately identifiable and significant.

For instance, let's assume a patient comes into the office with a splinter in his finger and your physician looks at the splinter and removes it and bills for a removal of foreign body CPT code.

By itself, you are not justified in billing a visit with a 25 modifier to it. But, if the physician has to determine when the last time the patient had a tetanus, determine whether a tetnus injection is warranted, obtain a new history on the patient and order any medications, you may have a low level E&M billable with a modifier 25.

A large percentage of the physicians I consult with are Osteopathic Physicians (D.O.s) and most of them perform OMT (Osteopathic Manipulative Therapy) on their patients. When a patient presents with a pain, the physician must use diagnostic skills to determine whether the pain is muscle related, orthopedic, psychological, injury related, stress related, etc...before being able to determine what treatment is applicable.

They document the history, exam and medical decision making and then they may decide to perform the OMT on the patient. Since the visit is obviously separately identifiable and significant, I encourage them to use the 25 modifier on those visits.

Now – most patients will need 2 or 3 Osteopathic treatments before the physician achieves the desired result, so they may tell the patient to return 3 or 4 days later for another treatment.

On that day, when the patient returns, the physician will do a cursory examination and abbreviated history before performing the OMT, but usually not significant enough to warrant a separate evaluation and management, so I do not recommend they charge a visit on those 2nd or 3rd visits. Usually! Now, sometimes the patient will bring up a new problem or new complaint during the visit. This may necessitate another office visit if it is significant and separately identifiable, so we may return to the scenario of using the 25 modifier. Each visit can be different in this respect.

Many office managers have convinced their physician that you need a different or separate diagnosis for the office visit when billing for a visit with a procedure on the same visit. While there may be some carriers that require this, I have never seen Medicaid or the major carriers require this and Medicare definitely does not. CMS Bureau of Policy Development sent a letter to all Regional Medicare Administrators that included:

*"As you know, we have a policy which does not permit payment for evaluation and management services performed on the same day as a minor procedural service, unless the evaluation and management service is a "documented, separately identifiable service." It has come to our attention that some carriers are not paying for such separately identifiable services unless they are "unrelated" to the procedural service. This is not correct. A documented, separately identifiable related service is to be paid for. We would define related as being caused or prompted by the same symptoms or conditions."*

So, if a carrier requires a different diagnosis for the procedure and evaluation and management service, you may want to remind them that CMS does not require this and they may be in violation of the 1974 ERISA law by not following the standards of the industry in this regard. You do not have to jump through all of the hoops that the carriers are trying to make you abide by, if you know the regulations and where to find them!

A mistake that is very common with primary care practices is that they under-code the level of service they are providing, in hopes that it will keep them off the radar screen at the carrier for auditing. That is comparable to driving 52 miles per hour on the interstate in a 70 mph zone to keep from getting a ticket. It is foolishness and it is costing the average primary care practice at least $60,000 a year in my opinion, based on performing hundreds of coding/billing audits on primary care practices for 25 years.

In fact, the offices that routinely under-code are leaving themselves wide open for Medicare Recovery Audit Contractor (RAC) audits since the auditors realize that offices doing that are also making other coding mistakes and they are easy to identify. CMS gathers data from every Medicare carrier, by locality and publishes this information to the Medicare carriers nationwide, so that an auditor can easily pull up an individual's coding patterns and compare it to the national averages.

Many managers and physicians mistakenly believe that Medicare auditors will compare how YOU code today to how you coded last quarter and if there is a marked difference, then they audit you. That is untrue. They compare your coding to the other physicians of your specialty and if you are coding much higher than everyone else, in a particular category, then they may flag you for an audit. If you're coding per the level of service that is medically necessary and that is clearly documented, then why would you care if they look at your charts or progress notes? If you're driving down the highway in a 55 mph zone and you're driving 55 mph and you see a highway patrol officer clocking your speed with a radar gun, do you slam on the brakes? If you do – then you're a moron that shouldn't be driving. Of course you don't, so why are you afraid of an auditor auditing your documentation?

If you're coding and billing correctly, then you have nothing to fear, so code it and document it appropriately from the beginning. It is utterly ridiculous, in my opinion, that physicians giving good medical care and taking good care of their patients should be intimidated into under-coding or down-coding their services.

My sister and her husband have 11 children living at home, ranging in ages from 1 to 18. If they followed the example set by the majority of physicians in this country, they would only claim 14 kids on their income tax so as to hopefully avoid an IRS audit. Your under-coding is equally stupid, so don't do it. Bill the level you're legally entitled to!

## When Doctor Doesn't Document Enough

A very common question that we receive is how to bill for a service when the doctor didn't document as much as is required by the 1995 or 1997 documentation guidelines. For instance, a new patient visit requires all 3 components (history, exam and medical decision making). If a physician only documents two, the question is asked whether the staff can bill an established patient visit (which only requires 2 of the 3).

If you talk to CMS personnel, you'll get a variety of answers ranging from using an established patient visit to an unlisted evaluation and management code (99499). My advice is that if the physician doesn't document the minimum requirements for the coding area (new patient visit, hospital admit, etc), then I do not give the physician any code to use.

If you hired a boy to mow your entire yard and he mowed only 2/3 of it because something he wanted to watch on television was coming on and he didn't have time, would you partially pay him? If a plumber comes to your home because your bathroom faucet was leaking water and he just slowed down the leak but didn't stop it, would you partially pay him? If your daughter did some of her chores, but not all of them, would you partially give her an allowance? If so — then you're not teaching your daughter to be responsible if you reward partial behavior. The same thing applies to giving your physician credit when they fail to document the components they need and should document.

## Linking Diagnosis Code To CPT Code

One of the most common reasons why claims are denied is that the diagnosis code used in block 24 on the claim does not justify the service being billed for in block 25 of the claim form.

The typical office, not using EMR, will have the physician mark the visit, lab tests, diagnostic tests and procedures rendered on the charge ticket (also called a superbill) and at the bottom of the form, write in 3 or 4 diagnosis. The person keypunching the claims into the computer is almost NEVER a physician, physician assistant or nurse practitioner and their medical/clinical knowledge is almost always OJT (on the job training). Some will even have had anatomy classes, but this person is now tasked with linking the correct diagnosis to the appropriate CPT or HCPCS code.

Some believe that because they are a CPC (Certified Procedural Coder) or CCS (Certified Coding Specialist) that they will naturally be able to link them – but that is basic hogwash in most cases. Yes, the person knows coding and they passed a test to prove they know coding, but they are not omnipotent or even clairvoyant in that they KNOW what the provider was thinking. While some will be really easy, such as the removal of impacted cerumen (69210) linked to diagnosis code 480.4 (impacted cerumen), others will be more complicated.

For instance, the lipid panel (80061) was ordered for which diagnosis or symptom? The APO Lipo A and B should be linked to which diagnosis?

The CBC could have been ordered due to an infection or the fact that the physician believes (as Medicare does) that everyone on long term chronic medications should have a CBC (complete blood count) routinely to monitor the effects of the medications. How is the biller, coder, keypuncher supposed to know what the physician is thinking?

There are usually 2 main ways for a physician or provider to link the diagnosis code to the procedure code, if not using an EMR. One way is to put a letter designation, such as A, B, or C next to the procedure or visit code marked on the superbill and the corresponding diagnosis gets the same letter designation. The other way (not my favorite) is for the physician or provider to draw a line from the diagnosis to the appropriate CPT code – but that usually starts looking like the yellow lines on your television when John Madden drawing on a screen while he's explaining "The tight end started to go to the right, but then was blocked, so the halfback, cut left and wasn't sure if the hole would open, so in confusion, he fumbled the ball and fumbling the ball is never a good thing, and that reminds me of the time that I picked up a fumble and fell down and went boom because my feet slid out on the wet turf and…".

If your providers are not linking the diagnosis to the procedures, in all likelihood, your claims are not reflective of the real reason why the provider performed the services, and that can definitely contribute to the denials you may be receiving. It doesn't take a lot to retrain your provider once the incentive (being paid) to do it right is made clear to them.

## Local Coverage Determinations (LCDs)

Since most providers are not absolutely clear as to what diagnosis must be on the claim to justify a procedure, lab test or diagnostic test, it would help your providers to have a list of the Local Coverage Determinations by Medicare. Not all carriers utilize Medicare's parameters but most do. If you're reading the PDF version, you can click on:

http://www.cms.hhs.gov/mcd/search.asp?from2=search.a
sp&

and your browser will open to the CMS LCD page. If you're reading the paperback version, type the above link into the address bar on your internet browser. LCDs list the coverage criteria, frequency of coverage, who may perform the service or diagnostic test, covered diagnosis or symptoms and other relevant payment information on most services.

For instance, if you want to bill for an EKG, you must have one of more than 200 specific diagnosis or symptoms on the claim for the carrier to indicate the EKG was medically necessary. Without it, the carriers will probably deny the claim. You can click on either NATIONAL or LOCAL determinations when you get to that website (I almost always click on local, since some states differ in the coverage issues on the same diagnostic service) and plug in the state and CPT code that you need the LCD for.

When Keith and I are performing the free telephone diagnostic analysis on practices, using Webex so that the client can see our computers, we show them the local coverage issues for their location and we have found that most physicians are not aware of them.

Interestingly, most of the office managers we have dealt with are also not familiar with how to access them and even more surprising is that many certified coders are not as well. Everyone billing for medical offices should be intimately familiar with how to pull up the LCDs for their area for every procedure or diagnostic test they perform. To not be familiar with how to access them, either through the CMS website or an updated coding program reflects very negatively on that person's ability to do their job properly. (You were warned that I'm not politically correct and that I do not dance around a point when a point has to be made).

Not only does the LCD indicate what diagnosis must be on the claim or the frequency of how often the service is covered, but it also lists the criteria for that state or locality as to the qualifications of the personnel performing the service. For instance, in Texas, anyone in the office can perform a spirometry on a patient as it's really simple. Florida Medicare has a different rule in that they require a Respiratory Therapist (or someone with similar certification or licensing) be the one that performs the service, and that means that every physician in Florida having their RN, LVN or MA perform the spirometry in their office is subject to recoupment and possible fines by Medicare.

Florida Medicare also requires specific certification (if it is not the physician, physician assistant or nurse practitioner performing it) for the person performing ABI (Ankle Brachial Indices). Most providers in Florida performing this service on their diabetic and hypertensive patients are not aware of the certification requirements for the technician, in spite of the fact that the Medicare LCD clearly indicates those requirements. Many physicians have figured out that it's best to have their nurse hook up the ABI brachial and ankle cuffs to the patient and do the blood pressure readings and the physician comes in and does the pulse Doppler on the ankle, so that they are complying with the Medicare requirements.

Those that are having their nurses do the entire test will be sorely disappointed when and if they are ever audited by a Recovery Audit Contractor.

The Local Coverage Determinations are also subject to change from time to time (usually at the whim of the Medicare carrier medical director for their state or locality), so it's a good idea to check these from time to time to make sure you're still compliant.

## Choosing The ICD-9 Code

The ICD-9-CM Coding Guidelines instruct physicians to report diagnoses based on test results, if available. Providers must comply with the following instructions in determining the appropriate diagnosis code for diagnostic test results.

♦ Use the ICD-9-CM code that describes the patient's diagnosis, symptom, complaint, condition or problem.

♦ Do not code suspected diagnosis.

♦ Use the ICD-9-CM code that is chiefly responsible for the item or service provided.

♦ Assign codes to the highest level of specificity. Use the fourth and fifth digits where applicable.

♦ Code a chronic condition as often as applicable to the patient's treatment.

♦ Code all documented conditions that coexist at the time of the visit that require or affect patient care or treatment.

If the physician has confirmed a diagnosis based on the results of the diagnostic test, the physician interpreting the test should code that diagnosis. The signs and/or symptoms that prompted ordering the test may be reported as additional diagnoses if they are not fully explained or related to the confirmed diagnosis.
The Medicare Carrier Manual, at CMS 30.61 says: "For outpatient encounters for diagnostic tests that have been interpreted by a physician, and the final report is available at the time of coding, code any confirmed or definitive diagnoses documented in the interpretation. Do not code related signs & symptoms as additional diagnoses".

This means that if you are billing for an ABI test because the patient has pain in the limb (ICD9 code 729.5), but the test clearly shows the patient has acute coronary occlusion without myocardial infarction (411.81), you should link the occlusion diagnosis code to the ABI code.

## ICD-10 Facts

There are about 2 billion encounters a year in the medical field. Currently, ICD-9 has about 13,000 codes and they are 3 to 5 digits long. ICD-10 (currently scheduled for October 1, 2010) will handle the same encounters with about 120,000 codes, but they will be 3 to 7 digits long. This will mean increased detail in the physician documentation.

Quin Buechner, an excellent consultant out of Wisconsin gave a great example: "one of the new I-10 codes is ONLY used when a patient has an open skull fracture and also open facial bone fractures and 3 types of intracranial hemorrhage and is unconscious for 24 hrs. and does not regain consciousness. And this accuracy has to be exactly documented and the payer really needs that detail, why? And the provider really is going to document that detail, without a fight, you bet? And this helps the patient, how? Also, how many errors have we seen where I and # 1 or O and # 0 are confused, yet I-10 uses both."

So, as you can tell, we are not in a hurry to bring ICD-10 online and you will need to schedule your staff and providers for a webinar (hopefully mine) or a seminar prior to October 1st, 2010. Yes, there are some people looking forward to ICD-10.

Their argument is that the increased details in the codes will provide better statistical data. My question, though, is "at what cost?".

I like what Quin said in an email: "Every one of the 500,000 coders will need retraining plus the providers (and the consultants who will be asked to train them). Computer upgrades and reprogramming is going to have to be done universally from Government to payer to practice, (since the fields for diagnosis only accepts up to 5 digits now). The HIPAA experience shows we really will be doing more than something simple like a small upgrade. Oh, by the way, the DRGs and APCs and other reimbursement systems will need to be rebuilt to accommodate the ICD-10."

A comprehensive, independent study by the Rand Corporation, commissioned by the government, estimated that the total costs of implementation were estimated at about $425 million to $1.15 billion in one-time costs for training and systems changes for providers, payers, and vendors, plus between $5 to $40 million per year in lost productivity. Can your practice afford that?

Yes, it's coming in October 2010 (unless they delay it again) and we can't change that − but is this really the answer to our problems or does it cause more problems than we should have?

I was talking to John Jackson (CEO of Intelicode and my friend), and he gave me a great quote. "If we are ready for ICD-10 by 2011, then it will be delayed beyond that. If we're not ready for ICD-10, then it will take place in 2011. It just makes sense to be ready for it". He is so right.

## When Is A Nurse Visit (99211) Appropriate?

This question arises quite often in seminars and in the consultations we perform for primary care offices. Typically, a nurse visit is charged when the hypertensive patient is following the doctor's orders and comes in to get a blood pressure check by the nurse.

You should bill a 99211 to the insurance and collect the co-pay or co-insurance from the patient at the time of service. The question about billing a 99211 often comes when the patient is coming in for an injection (either a typical antibiotic or even an allergy injection).

Many (not I) feel that it is justified to bill for a 99211 instead of the administration of the injection because it takes the time of the nurse, but then.... that is what an administration of injection (96372, 90471, 95115, etc) is for.

Keep in mind that we should always use the code that "best describes" the services being rendered. If those services have us swabbing the patient's arm or buttock with an alcohol swab and then poke them with a needle to get something other than Dr. Pepper into their body, and then put a Snoopy bandage on them, then we should bill out for the administration of the injection code without an office visit (99211). That should include whatever normal conversation is had when an injection is given, such as asking the patient how they are feeling, whether they are allergic to what we're giving them, whether they are terrified of needles, who was voted off last night on American Idol, etc.

On the other hand, if the patient shows up for an injection and it's obvious to the staff (nurse, MA, LVN, LPN or whomever) that there are problems that require them to get a blood pressure check, pulse recording, temperature, etc... then a visit would be justified in addition to the administration of an injection and it should be billed. The problem will be that the National Correct Coding Initiative edits (NCCI) bundles the 99211 into the 96372 (since January 1st, 2009). This means that you will NOT be paid for both, per Medicare or any other carrier using the NCCI edits.

A 99212 and a 96372 is not bundled together, so if the physician deems it medically necessary to enter the room with the patient and documents the appropriate level of history, exam and medical decision making for a 99212, then you may be paid for both of these codes.

Conversely, do not bill for services due to the fact you did it and not due to medical necessity. This happens when the staff and doctors tell me they are getting the vitals so they can charge for a nurse visit. That is exactly the OPPOSITE of what it should be and it IS considered to be fraudulent or abusive billing practices.

They are doing the service so that they CAN bill for it. It should be that they are doing the service for medically necessary reasons and THAT justifies the billing. A good example would be the billing for routine venipuncture when you have the patient come in only to get blood drawn for a lab test ordered by the doctor. That should be billed out as a 36415 (recommended fee is $15) and perhaps even a 99000 if you are preparing the specimen to be sent to an outside lab.

I do not believe a simple blood draw justifies the 99211 simply because you may be routinely getting a blood pressure check before the venipuncture.

If you are doing the BP check due to a medically necessary reason such as hypertension, orthostatic hypotension, lightheadedness, dizziness, etc... then it is justified – but not routinely for all blood draws.

If you do routinely charge for 99211 because you are doing blood pressure checks during all blood draws, you can probably expect to be audited within the next 4 years as Medicare, Recovery Audit Contractors (RAC) and CMS is watching for this practice.

There is not one complete source for the correct use of 99211. What follows is a compilation of the rules from Medicare, Medicaid and CMS. Most payers have also agreed with the following list.

1. The face to face provider must be an employee, contractor or leased employee.

2. There must be direct supervision (i.e. billing physician in the suite) for services.

3. The patient must be seen first by the Physician/Practitioner, so that a plan of care is established.

4. There must be an order for the service.

5. There must be a documented rationale for medical necessity.

6. There must be a date and clear identifier/signature of the face to face provider.

7. 99211 is a -25 modifier eligible code so that other services can be billed when the use of the modifier is allowable, although the NCCI edits may not allow both to be paid.

8. 99211 must never be used if there is a more accurate code to report the services.

9. 99211 can be used for a person-to-person, office medication refill IF the Physician/Practitioner is providing on-going management for the patient.

10. 99211 may be used for drawing labs for immediate in-house protocol or order and a management change happens due to the lab testing (as in the case with PT/INR that will be discussed in the next section)

11. 99211 can be used for short patient teaching sessions that are medically necessary or reflect a medication change.

12. 99211 can be used to report a flush of a port when not therapy is done.

13. 99211 can be used for blood pressure check that are ordered and are medically necessary. Under Medicare rules a 99211 can be used for PT and PTTs, if:

>   1. face to face medication management is provided, there is documentation to establish a need for clinical evaluation and management of significant new symptoms or clearly demonstrating how the relevant lab information was used to modify therapy,

2.  current medications are listed with notation of compliance,

3.  an indication is documented showing the Physician or Practitioner's evaluation of the labs and recommendation management recommendation &

4.  clear identity and credentials of the staff and Physician or Practitioner are shown..

## 99211 & PT/INR

CPT code 99211 is the lowest level evaluation and management (E/M) service and does not require a physician face-to-face encounter with the patient. However, it does require direct physician supervision (i.e. the supervising physician must be present in the office when the service is rendered) of the ancillary staff who are conducting the face-to-face encounter. Services billed to Medicare under CPT code 99211 must be reasonable and necessary for the diagnosis and treatment of an illness or injury. This would include appropriately performed and documented anticoagulation management.
The following represents the guidelines that would be used in review of these charges as well as the errors that have previously been found on carrier or Comprehensive Error Rate Testing reviews.

## 99211 for Anticoagulation Management "Do's"

- Documenting the patient's indication for anticoagulant therapy, current dose, protime and INR results
- Assessing the patient in-person for signs and symptoms of bleeding/adverse effects to anticoagulant therapy
- Assessing the patient for changes in health status that may impact or account for fluctuations in lab results (for example, new or changed medications that may cause a drug interaction with the anticoagulant therapy)
- Providing medically necessary education as needed based on the patient's individual circumstances
- Documenting the identity of the ancillary staff performing this service "incident to" the supervising physician
- Documenting the identity of the billing physician who was notified of results, gave orders, and provided direct supervision.

## 99211 for Anticoagulation Management "Don'ts"

- Billing for 99211 when the in-person encounter with the patient was only for the diagnostic test

- Billing for 99211 for telephone care, i.e. instructions on changing dose, assessment, and/or education
- Billing for 99211 when the only documentation would be vital signs, the patient's current and future dose of anticoagulant, and when lab work is to be repeated
- Billing for 99211 when direct physician supervision is not met or is not by the physician treating the patient's medical problem requiring anticoagulant therapy (i.e. as seen in some "Coumadin ® clinic" scenarios)
- Billing for 99211 based on the delivery of repetitive education that does not serve the medical needs of the individual patient

The above was in their newsletter at
http://www.cignagovernmentservices.com/partb/pubs/ne
ws/2007/0907/cope6426.html

So—while the 1997 and 1995 documentation guidelines only require chief complaint and 1 HPI, without any ROS or PFSH or exam elements (99211 is the only code that doesn't require the 2 of 3), this Medicare carrier requires that you document the information in the left column.

You may wish to review this with the nurse, MA or whomever in your office does the INR (International Normalized Ratio) visits in your office to make sure your documentation would support you if you're ever audited. We do not recommend you stop charging for the visits — but we do recommend you follow these guidelines—just to be safe.

It is also not appropriate to bill for an office visit with the physician and then to bill for a separate nurse visit on the same day because the nurse is doing something different than the physician. The nurse's services would be deemed to be an integral component of the office visit billed by the physician or provider.

Along the same lines, you cannot bill for multiple visits in one day, regardless of the place of service. Medicare's rules state that physicians in the same group practice who are in the same specialty must bill and be paid as though they were a single physician.

If more than one E&M (face-to-face) service is provided on the same day to the same patient by the same physician or more than one physician in the same specialty in the same group, only one E&M service may be reported unless the E&M services are for unrelated problems. Instead of billing separately, the physicians should select a level of service representative of the combined visits and submit the appropriate code for that level.

## Using Time To Determine Level Of Code

If more than 50% of the visit is spent in counseling and/or coordination of care for a medically justified reason, then you do not have to worry about documenting the history, exam & medical decision making, as long as the physician or provider appropriately documents the total time, time spent on the counseling and/or coordination of care and what was discussed. This happens in just about every office and in many; it may happen multiple times a day. The CPT book and Medicare lists the "normal" times for office/outpatient visits as:

| | | | |
|---|---|---|---|
| 99201 | 10 minutes | 99211 | 5 minutes |
| 99202 | 20 minutes | 99212 | 10 minutes |
| 99203 | 30 minutes | 99213 | 15 minutes |
| 99204 | 40 minutes | 99214 | 25 minutes |
| 99205 | 60 minutes | 99215 | 40 minutes |

Medicare does not require that you document the start-stop times when documenting the counseling/coordination of care, although it may be a good idea to get into the habit so that you cannot be challenged in an audit.

A perfect example of when the visit will be dominated by counseling is when you have a patient that was in a week ago and clinical lab tests were run on them and today they come in for the results.

You're not going to do a new history or a new exam, although you will do some new decision making, but the majority of the visit will be counseling. If you're telling a patient they have diabetes, then you're spending at least another 15 to 25 minutes going over the diabetes, what it is, how it's treated, what ramifications they have, what symptoms to watch for, complications, what they can and cannot do, etc...

You may even be coordinating care with a DME company or a supplier of home glucose testing. The only way you can effectively code that visit is by utilizing the counseling/coordination of care method of billing and that requires you document the total time, the amount of time YOU (the provider) spent with the patient counseling or the time YOU spent coordinating care with another caregiver or supplier or ordering DME, etc... Always count the "normal" times as the MINIMUM so that if you spent 21 minutes, you qualified for a 99213 and not a 99214 as you do not round to the nearest time. If you spent 35 minutes, it would be a 99214 and not a 99215 since you didn't quite make it to the 40 minute mark.

You can and should use the counseling and/or coordination of care billing rules with any carrier unless they have posted that they do not ascribe to this, but we've yet to see any that have not adopted this type of documentation yet. There may be some that exist, but we're not aware of them as of the printing of this book.

Only the CPT codes that list the "normal" times in the CPT codebook allow using the counseling and/or coordination of care documentation, and those include

> New and Established Office/Outpatient visits (99201 – 99215),
> Out-patient and In-Patient Consultation Codes (99241 – 99255),
> In-Patient Hospital Initial Care (usually called Admits – 99221 - 99223) and
> In-Patient Hospital Daily Care codes (99231 – 99233) and
> Skilled Nursing Home coding (99304-99310).

Emergency room codes (99281-99285) do not have normal times associated with them in either the CPT codebook or the Medicare Carrier Manual, so you may not use time to determine the level of coding in the Emergency Department series of coding.

## Prolonged Service Coding (99354 – 99357)

There will be instances where a physician or provider will need to spend 30 or more minutes beyond the normal time with a patient for a medically necessary reason. That is why the CPT developed the prolonged service codes 99354 – 99357 for face-to-face prolonged services. They have additional codes for non face-to-face service, but since Medicare and most private/commercial carriers are not paying for those, we won't discuss them.

At least 80% of the practices today are not using the prolonged service codes and of those that are billing for them, a fair number of those are not billing for them correctly. In some instances, they are using the prolonged service codes WITHOUT billing for the associated evaluation and management (visit) codes and that is not correct.

The prolonged service codes are 'add-on' or extra codes to be billed in addition to the visit to compensate the physician for the extra 30 minutes or more being spent on the patient's condition.

In the instance where you have a group practice and two or more physicians of the same specialty, in that group practice, sees a patient more than once a day, you cannot bill multiple E&M visits, but you can combine the time that was documented by the physicians on the medically necessary services and if that exceeds, by 30 minutes, the normal times shown for that category of coding, you can use the prolonged service code to compensate for the additional time.

This typically happens on a day when a patient is admitted into the hospital in the morning, after an office visit. Let's assume that Dr. A saw the patient in the office and spent 30 minutes examining the patient, running tests, etc. and then decided to admit the patient to the hospital. Dr. B (also same specialty) goes by the hospital and sees the patient at lunchtime and visits with the patient's family garnering more information and spends another 30 minutes and at the end of the day, Dr. A stops by and spends 30 minutes with the patient and their family, reviewing tests, etc...

This would give you 90 minutes total time spent today, and since you cannot expect to be paid for an office visit on the same day as a hospital admit (also called initial inpatient care), you would look at the times shown in the CPT book and Medicare Carrier Manual.

You find:

> 99221          30 minutes
> 99222          50 minutes
> 99223          70 minutes

If the history, exam and medical decision making for today's visit justifies a 99222, then it takes 80 minutes to exceed the normal time by 30 minutes, giving you a 99356 with the 99222.   If the history, exam and medical decision making was at a 99223 level, then it would take 100 minutes to exceed the 99223 by 30 minutes, allowing you to bill the 99356.

Note that 99355 and 99357 are add-on codes to the prolonged service in that they add another 30 minutes on to the additional time over 30 minutes.  The codes are:

> 99354 Outpatient  Face-to-Face  Prolonged  Service Initial 30 minutes
> 99355 Outpatient – Each additional 30 minutes over 99354
> 99356 Inpatient  Face-to-Face  Prolonged  Service Initial 30 minutes
> 99357 Inpatient – Each additional 30 minutes over 99356

Physicians may count only the duration of direct face-to-face contact between the provider and the patient (whether the service was continuous or not) beyond the typical/average time of the visit code billed to determine whether prolonged services can be billed and to determine the prolonged services codes that are allowable. In the case of prolonged office services, time spent by office staff with the patient, or time the patient remains unaccompanied in the office cannot be billed.

In the case of prolonged hospital services, time spent reviewing charts or discussion of a patient with house medical staff and not with direct face-to-face contact with the patient, or waiting for test results, for changes in the patient's condition, for end of a therapy, or for use of facilities cannot be billed as prolonged services.

It has to be face-to-face time with the provider (physician or mid level) and the patient and does not count nurse time, Medical Assistant time, etc...

If the entire visit is spent counseling and/or coordination of care or if the level of visit is being determined by the counseling and/or coordination of care, the prolonged service code can only be appended to the highest level of code in that category (99205, 99215, 99223, 99333, etc) and not the lower level codes, per Medicare Transmittal 1490, dated July 1, 2008.

Typically, Medicare's allowed amount for the 99354 code runs from about $87 to $105, so this definitely is worth billing when your physician or provider spends the time with the patient and documents it properly.

## Initial Inpatient Care (Admits)

For years, people have been referring to billing for hospital admits and the truth is that no one pays for an "admit" or H&P (History & Physical). The CPT codes do not reference Admits or H&Ps either and neither does Medicare.

On January 1st of 2010, Medicare even changed how they pay for the initial inpatient care codes 99221, 99222 and 99223 – even though not all other carriers have adopted Medicare's new guidelines in this area.

In years past, one physician was allowed to bill for the initial inpatient care code and   all other providers billed for subsequent, daily care (per diem) codes 99231, 99232 or 99233 when they saw the patient in the hospital (except for consultations – which will be discussed later).

Medicare has ALWAYS required that a face-to-face (or face-to-something-else for Proctologists) visit between the provider and the patient take place IN the hospital if the initial inpatient care codes would be billed.

Consequently, many offices have been in the habit of the physician seeing the patient in the office and admitting the patient to the hospital FROM the office with a phone call, without physically going to the hospital.   When Medicare audited practices for this and discovered the physician or provider never actually took their posterior to the hospital to see the patient IN the facility on that day, they've retroactively denied the claim and demanded recoupment.

This has caused a problem for many offices and the fact that the physician, the biller, the certified coder and the office manager did not KNOW that the initial inpatient care code had to be rendered IN the place where the place of service denoted, was not a valid excuse.

When you use the 99221, 99222 or 99223 code, you are using the place of service 21 code, so it makes sense that the service would be rendered there, in the same fashion as the home visits have a place of service 12 and you cannot bill for the home visits unless you see the patient in their home.

Again, as of January 1, 2010, Medicare changed their rules (and some private/mangled care plans have followed their lead) so that every physician seeing a patient in the hospital, for the first time during that hospital stay, should use the Initial Inpatient care codes 99221, 99222 or 99223 for the first visit. They should then use the daily care per diem codes 99231 – 99233 for each visit after the first.
The question comes up with group practices where more than one physician will see the patient in the hospital and whether each physician should use the initial inpatient care code for each first visit.

Medicare (and most other carriers, if not all) consider every physician in a group practice – in the same specialty to be a clone of each other physician in that they have identical DNA. In other words, if 3 family physicians are in a group practice, then it doesn't matter which of the 3 sees the patient, because it is as if all three saw the patient.

If a second physician of the same specialty in the same practice sees a patient in the hospital, you treat it as if the first physician saw them again as they are considered to be the same person since they are of the same specialty and same group practice (same tax identification qualifies as same practice).

To clarify, let's assume that Family Practitioner Doctor Black saw a hospital patient on Monday for the first time, so Dr. H will bill a 99222 for instance. His partner, Family Practitioner Doctor White sees the same patient on Tuesday, making rounds, so Dr. White cannot bill an initial care code since Dr. Black did, so he bills a daily care code from the 99231-99233 range.

On Wednesday, their third partner, Dr. Brown sees the patient and again, it's from the 99231-99233 range – even though this is the first time that Dr. Brown saw the patient in the hospital, because Black, White & Brown are considered to have the same DNA so they are the same person, per Medicare. (Wouldn't it be nice if everyone in our country was like this and just called themselves American instead of everyone wanting to claim some kind of privilege with hyphenation because their ancestors came from Europe or Africa or Mexico?) Hey – don't freak out – you know the name of this book is "Unfiltered", so put your big girl panties on and live with it.

Yes, you can bill for the Prolonged Service codes with the hospital daily care codes 99231-99233, since they have time associated with them, just as you can select the level of hospital daily care by using the time spent on counseling and/or coordination of care.

You can and should ALSO bill for any procedures performed in the hospital on the patients and don't expect your billing staff to automatically know what YOU did while you were at the hospital. They may be great with intuition, but they are not at the hospital with you. Your billing staff do not know if you

> ➤ started an arterial line,
> ➤ gave an injection into a joint or a trigger point or
> ➤ treated a burn or
> ➤ destroyed a lesion or
> ➤ treated a bedsore or
> ➤ removed impacted cerumen or
> ➤ interpreted an X-ray or EKG

while there – unless you tell them so.

I accompanied a physician to the hospital about 20 years ago and made rounds with him (this was prior to HIPAA) wearing a smock and taking notes, prior to returning to his office where he saw patients. At the end of the day, I had noted $504 in missed charges that he didn't note and he was better at coding than probably 90% of the physicians I've seen since then.

If he missed that much, how much is YOUR physician missing? It may behoove you to accompany your doctor once or twice to educate your doctor what they may be missing. Even if it's only half of what I found with that doctor, you're still looking at $65,000 a year in missed income.

If you're not using an Out-Of-Office charge card, to indicate what they did, what level of service was billed, etc... (for those not tied in to the hospital EMR system), then you're probably losing at least $65,000 a year.

It may be twice that if you're GUESSING what level of E&M to bill. Your physician or provider should be the one telling the billing staff which level they provided, since the billing staff usually doesn't have easy access to the progress note to help the provider pick it. If your provider is too lazy to pick their own code, the safest way to do so is to choose the lowest level and then point out the difference in income their laziness is costing them. One visit a day billed at 99231 instead of 99232 (Using Medicare's allowed amounts on a 5 day work week) equates to $7,533 a year on average lost income.

If your physician sees an average of 3 patients a day, that's about $22,000 a year in lost income because of the under-coding. You should always code the appropriate level of service that you're giving and documenting.

If you are using an out of office charge card, you may be having to get the physician's keys each day and go out to the parking lot to find the cards laying between the seats, in the doctor's smock pocket, etc... It is definitely worth finding those cards as there is a lot of income to be gained from getting the information.

Some may think that the "bundling" rule that includes the office visit on the same day as an admit is a Medicare rule only —but it is also a CPT rule.

As it says: "When the patient is admitted to the hospital as an inpatient in the course of an encounter in another site of service (eg, hospital emergency department, observation status in a hospital, physician's office, nursing facility) all evaluation and management services provided by that physician in conjunction with that admission are considered part of the initial hospital care when performed on the same date as the admission. The inpatient care level of service reported by the admitting physician should include the services related to the admission he/she provided in the other sites of service as well as in the inpatient setting.

## Modifier AI

• The principal physician of record will append modifier "-AI" (as in Actively Involved) as the Principal Physician of Record, to the E/M code when billed. This modifier will identify the physician who oversees the patient's care from all other physicians who may be furnishing specialty care. All other physicians who perform an initial evaluation on this patient will bill only the E/M code for the complexity level performed.

(The AI modifier is only informational and does not change the amount that will be paid)

• However, claims that include the "-AI" modifier on codes other than the initial hospital and nursing home visit codes (i.e., subsequent care codes or outpatient codes) will not be rejected and returned to the physician or provider.

• For patients receiving hospital outpatient observation services who are not subsequently admitted to the hospital as in-patients, physicians should report CPT codes 99217-99220. In the event another physician evaluation is necessary, the physician who provides the additional evaluation bills the office or other outpatient visit codes when they provide services to the patient.

## Admit From Emergency Room To Inpatient Hospital

You're requested by the ER physician to come into the ER to render an opinion. You examine the patient and determine the best course of action is to admit the patient into the hospital, so how do you bill for the E&M?

Since Medicare stopped paying for consultations (even in the E.R.), for Medicare patients, you can either bill the ER visit (99281 – 99285) or the proper way is to bill for the initial inpatient care (99221 – 99223) – but remember that you MUST see the patient in the in-patient facility in order to bill for the initial-in-patient codes.

None of the carriers pay for both E/M services, if rendered on the same date and the ER visit is related to the reason for the hospital admission.

The Medicare Carrier Manual says: "When the patient is admitted to the hospital via another site of service (e.g., hospital emergency department, physician's office, skilled nursing facility), all services provided by the physician in conjunction with that admission are considered part of the initial hospital care when performed on the same date as the admission."

Therefore, if your physician performs the Emergency Room Visit and the hospital admit, you'll bill for the initial inpatient care (admit) as that bundles the emergency room visit.

There are also some that believe that only one emergency room visit code (99281-99285) can be billed on one date and that if your family physician is called to the hospital emergency room to see the patient by the ER doctor, that you cannot bill an ER visit code. That is not true. The ER physician is one specialty code and your Family Physician or Internist is a different specialty, so both can bill the insurance or Medicare with the same series of codes since they are not of the same specialty and in the same group practice.

## Admit To Critical Care From E.R.

If you're in the emergency room for long, you'll run into the circumstance where you end up admitting a patient from the ER directly into critical care area in the hospital, regardless if it is in the ICU, CCU, PICU, etc... This is where is vital that the physician document the time spent on everything they do while taking care of the critically ill patient.

The time spent on procedures, such as supervising or performing CPR has to be deducted from the total critical care time so that the physician isn't being paid twice for the same time increment. The same thing with any other procedures the physician is doing during critical care, such as tracheotomy, suturing, etc.

A critical illness or injury acutely impairs one or more vital organ systems such that there is a high probability of imminent or life threatening deterioration in the patient's condition.

Medicare and other carriers do not permit a physician to be paid for a hospital admit rendered at the same time as critical care services, so you have to decide whether you wish to bill for an initial inpatient care (admit) or a critical care charge.

Let's examine Medicare allowed amounts in one locality so that we can see which pays best:

> 99221        $ 90.78
> 99222        $122.94
> 99223        $180.58
> 99291        $206.12
> 99292        $102.87

Ok, from these numbers, it is pretty evident that billing for critical care is much more lucrative than billing initial inpatient care, so if you spend 30 minutes or longer on the patient's critical condition, you should bill for the critical care and give the hospital admit to the patient for free. Don't forget to bill for the CPR (92950 = $167.73) or trach (31600 = $373.28) or whatever else you do, because EVERYTHING is not bundled into the critical care codes, as one might imagine (or someone may mistakenly tell you).

Medicare says: "When a hospital inpatient or office/outpatient evaluation and management service (E/M) are furnished on a calendar date at which time the patient does not require critical care and the patient subsequently requires critical care both the critical Care Services (CPT codes 99291 and 99292) and the previous E/M service may be paid on the same date of service.

Hospital emergency department services are not paid for the same date as critical care services when provided by the same physician to the same patient. During critical care management of a patient those services that do not meet the level of critical care shall be reported using an inpatient hospital care service with CPT Subsequent Hospital Care using a code from CPT code range 99231 – 99233."

## Critical Care In Any Place Of Service

It is a common misconception that you can only bill for critical care when the patient is in the hospital in an ICU area. That is about as factual as Al Gore saying that he helped invent the internet while in the Congress (since it was invented 4 years before he made it TO Congress) or his claims of global warming. You can render and bill for critical care in any place of service.

The only requirement is that the patient is CRITICAL (A critical illness or injury acutely impairs one or more vital organ systems such that there is a high probability of imminent or life threatening deterioration in the patient's condition) and your provider (physician or mid level) spent at least 30 minutes working on the CRITICAL condition.

Medicare says that the critical care services encompass both treatment of "vital organ failure" and "prevention of further life threatening deterioration of the patient's condition." Therefore, although critical care may be delivered in an emergency (patient stops breathing or threatens to vote for a liberal), this is not a requirement for providing critical care service.

The treatment and management of the patient's condition, while not necessarily emergent, shall be required, based on the THREAT of imminent deterioration (i.e., the patient shall be critically ill or injured at the time of the physician's visit).

Providing medical care to a critically ill patient should not be automatically deemed to be a critical care service for the sole reason that the patient is critically ill or injured. While more than one physician may provide critical care services to a patient during the critical care episode of an illness or injury each physician must be managing one or more critical illness(es) or injury(ies) in whole or in part.

As an example, about 8 years ago, while performing a full fee, code analysis of a doctor in New Orleans, I noticed that he had billed for 4 critical care charges in the previous month, so I looked at his records to make sure he had documented the critical care appropriately.

I then brought this to his attention, and pointed out that a Podiatrist trimming nails of a patient in the ICU could NOT be billed as critical care, in spite of how long, ugly and thick the nails were. The nails were not contributing to the patient's critical condition.

The same thing applies to the family physician who has handed the care of a patient's pulmonary collapse to a Pulmonologist. The Family Physician may be taking care of other things, but if the FP is not directly taking care of a critical condition, then the FP should NOT be billing for critical care – regardless where the physician is seeing the patient. Your FP may need to be billing for regular hospital visits, even though the patient is in the ICU.

In fact, this warning extends to the regular hospital floor as well. If your physician has turned over the care to the Orthopedic doctor and there is not another condition that your Family Physician is treating (diabetes, hypertension, hyperlipidemia, cough, etc) and the only condition is orthopedic and the Orthopedic Surgeon is taking care of the bones, then you shouldn't be billing for any visit as there is no medical necessity. Your doctor may wish to stop by and pick up some flowers as no medical necessity means no payment.

Your doctor doesn't have to only count the time spent hovering over the patient in the bed. For example, time spent reviewing laboratory test results or discussing the critically ill patient's care with other medical staff in the unit or at the nursing station on the floor may be reported as critical care, even when it does not occur at the bedside, if this time represents the doctor's or mid level's full attention to the management of the critically ill/injured patient.

Note that Physician Assistants and Nurse Practitioners can also render and bill for critical care. You must bill those services under their own number within the group – but not under incident-to.

The time with the patient's family may or may not be counted in the critical care time, depending on the circumstances. To count, consider whether

1. The patient is unable or incompetent to participate in giving history and/or making treatment decisions

2. There is necessity to have the discussion (e.g., "no other source was available to obtain a history" or "because the patient was deteriorating so rapidly I needed to immediately discuss treatment options with the family",

3. There are medically necessary treatment decisions for which the discussion was needed, and

4. You documented a summary in the medical record that supports the medical necessity of the discussion

All other family discussions, no matter how lengthy, may not be additionally counted towards critical care. Telephone calls to family members and or surrogate decision-makers may be counted towards critical care time, but only if they meet the same criteria as described in the aforementioned paragraph.

There are 2 CPT codes (99291 & 99292) to use for critical care services and you are not allowed to use the second one (99292) on a claim that does not also have the first code (99291). The CPT critical care codes 99291 and 99292 are used to report the total duration of time spent by a physician providing critical care services to a critically ill or critically injured patient, even if the time spent by the physician on that date is not continuous. Non-continuous time for medically necessary critical care services may be aggregated.

Reporting CPT code 99291 is a prerequisite to reporting CPT code 99292. Physicians of the same specialty within the same group practice bill and are paid as though they were a single physician.

To Medicare, it's as if each of the doctors in your group (of the same specialty) all share the same DNA, so when trying to figure out whether a different doctor can bill, think of the DNA and you'll probably answer your own question.

| Less than 30 min. | 99232 or 99233 or other appropriate E/M code |
|---|---|
| 30 - 74 minutes | 99291 x 1 |
| 75 - 104 minutes | 99291 x 1 and 99292 x 1 |
| 105 - 134 minutes | 99291 x1 and 99292 x 2 |
| 135 - 164 minutes | 99291 x 1 and 99292 x 3 |

Since these are TIMED codes, the physician's documentation must clearly indicate how much time was spent by the physician on the patient's critical care. The time by the nurse, medical assistant, transcriptionist, receptionist, or anyone else doesn't count. Only the provider's time counts.

As I said earlier, you can render critical care in your office – and that happens from time to time when you have a patient go into cardiac arrest, stop breathing or have other critical conditions in your office and as long as your provider spends AT LEAST 30 minutes working on the patient's critical condition before the patient is transported to the hospital (or elsewhere), you should look at the critical care codes.

The following services when performed on the day a physician bills for critical care are included in the critical care service and should not be reported separately:

- Interpretation of cardiac output measurements (CPT 93561, 93562);
- Chest x-rays, professional component (CPT 71010, 71015, 71020);
- Blood draw for specimen (CPT 36415);

- Blood gases, and information data stored in computers (e.g., ECGs, blood pressures, hematologic data-CPT 99090);
- Gastric intubation (CPT 43752, 91105);
- Pulse oximetry (CPT 94760, 94761, 94762);
- Temporary transcutaneous pacing (CPT 92953);
- Ventilator management (CPT 94002 – 94004, 94660, 94662); and
- Vascular access procedures (CPT 36000, 36410, 36415, 36591, 36600).

No other procedure codes are bundled into the critical care services. Therefore, other medically necessary procedure codes may be billed separately.

# Outpatient (24 - 48 Hour) Observation Admits/Visits

There are 3 main billing scenarios when you place a patient into observation:

1. A patient who is there for less than 8 hours
2. A patient who is admitted to observation & sent home the same date, &
3. A patient whose stay spans more than one date

## Patient Is In Observation For Less Than 8 Hours:

When a patient receives observation care for less than 8 hours on the same calendar date, the Initial Observation Care, from CPT code range 99218 – 99220, shall be billed by the physician ordering the observation stay. You will not bill an Observation Care Discharge Service code 99217 for the short term observation patient.

## Patient In Observation More than 8 Hours, But Discharged Same Date

In this case, you'll use the same codes as if you admitted the patient in-patient and discharged them the same date, as codes 99234, 99235 & 99236 denote an admit/discharge same date from either in-patient or out-patient observation.

## Patient In Observation Over More Than One Date

The physician ordering the observation care will bill the 99218, 99219 or 99220 code for the first date, making sure that all other E&M services that physician provided on that date is considered when choosing the correct code. A physician cannot bill for an ER visit or an office visit on the same day as an Initial Observation code

99218-20.

If the patient is NOT discharged on the second date, the physician will bill the office/outpatient visit codes 99211 – 99215 on the second date. Medicare's new policy took effect on January 4, 2010, regarding observation visits.

*A physician may not bill for more than one outpatient visit code on the 2nd date*, regardless of how many visits were made, so all of the related E&M services will be considered when choosing which level of code in the 99211 through 99215 series of codes. On the date the patient is discharged home, the physician should bill 99217, which also includes any other related E&M services done on that date, so you cannot bill for an out-patient visit and a discharge on the same day.

Often, the physician may decide the patient's condition worsened and admit the patient into in-patient status on the 2nd or 3rd date the patient is in observation. In that circumstance, you'll usually bill a 99221 or 99222 (level 1 and 2 of initial inpatient care codes) and not bill an observation discharge. As usual, the initial inpatient care code includes any related E&M services performed on that date.

The reason I did not list 99223 as "usually" being used in that circumstance (although it may be) is because most physicians are NOT performing a new complete review of systems and a new physical exam on the patient that they have seen at least twice in the past 24 hours and you always want to code the level of service actually performed and documented.

You also need to be aware the hospital may ask your physician to retroactively change the initial inpatient care (admit) date back to the date when the physician placed the patient into the observation. I do NOT recommend you allow the hospital to negate the observation dates as that would be fraudulent billing. In fact, Medicare Carrier Manual 30.6 clearly says the date of the initial inpatient care should be the date on the claim.

## Hospital Discharge

There are 3 different hospital discharge codes. Two of them are used for discharging the patient from the inpatient status (99238 & 99239) and one is used when discharging the patient from outpatient observation status (99217).

All three codes require a face-to-face with the patient, by the provider, on the date of discharge as these are not telephone discharge codes. The hospital discharge normally includes:

- Final examination(s),
- Discussion of hospital stay with patient and/or family,
- instructions for continuing care to all relevant caregivers,
- preparation of discharge record,
- prescriptions,
- home health coordination,
- DME orders, and
- referrals forms,

If the physician spends 31 minutes or longer, and documents the time, code 99239 should be billed. This code does not require start and stop times, although that is usually a good idea and will shut up an auditor quickly as it is incontrovertible proof that the provider documented.

The 99217 code should be used when discharging patients from a outpatient observation bed of the hospital.

A fellow consultant, Seth Canterbury in Florida, wrote: "99217 (like 99238/9) doesn't require or have any key components to meet. CPT specifically said that "No documentation guidelines were developed specifically for discharge services". The descriptions for the discharge codes say that they include such things as a final exam of patient/instructions for continuing care, but none of these individual components are required for any particular discharge service, as not all of them will not all be necessary on every discharge.

For example, a physician may come to work, and after reviewing a patient's labs/other values obtained overnight, decide that a reason for ongoing hospitalization no longer exists.

No real history is taken from the patient other than a cursory "So how are we feeling today?," (to which the patient says "Fine—I wanted to go home yesterday") and no physical exam is necessary in the doctor's eyes, as the patient's condition is not one that lends itself especially to physical exam anyway (especially not once it has reached the point at which it is almost fully resolved.)

He does likely look at the vitals from the last nursing assessment, but being normal as they've been for over 24 hours now, doesn't choose to create an "Exam" portion of his discharge note just to reference this fact. He informs the patient of the good overnight results and that they will be going home soon.

Medicare just requires that a face-to-face service be rendered. It has never contradicted CPT and required that certain amounts of the three key components that apply to other E/M services must be rendered with discharge services."

## Hospital Discharge & Nursing Home Admit On Same Day

Occasionally, you will have a patient leave the hospital and be admitted into a Skilled Nursing Facility (SNF) or a Nursing Home (NH) on the same date.

If the physician (in this case − it would have to be a physician and not a P.A. or N.P.) actually goes to the SNF or NH to see the patient on the same date, then you can and should bill for the hospital discharge (99238, 99239 or 99217) and the Initial Inpatient SNF or NH visit on the same date.

If you do, you will need to file the two services on different claims, as it is not possible to have services in two non office locations on the same claim as block 32 indicates where the service took place. One claim for the hospital discharge will either be with place of service 21 (in-patient hospital) or 22 (out-patient hospital), while the second claim will have place of service 31 (SNF) or 32 (NH).

It is required that the physician actually see the patient face-to-face in both places of service if you are billing for both services.

## Pronouncing Death – Signing Certificate

Contrary to their previous policy, when CMS was known as HCFA, CMS now states that All E/M services except where specifically stated (e.g., care plan oversight which is a monthly summary) require a face-to-face interaction between the physician and the patient. The discharge service is a face-to-face Evaluation and Management (E/M) service.

As required for other E&M codes, the discharge day management does not have the elements of history, exam, and medical decision-making. The doctor or NPP uses this final visit as appropriate, for a final examination, discussion of problems, instructions, coordination of care with other caregivers, such as HHS, DME, writing prescriptions and follow-up. A provider may choose to bill a subsequent hospital visit service code instead of a discharge service code. The provider is not required to bill a discharge day management service, although it is financially sound to do so.

The discharge day management service is a time-based service. In order to support services that require greater than 30 minutes (codes 99239 and 99316) the total time spent must be documented. If the time is not documented, payment is allowed for the lower level services (99238 and 99315).

A discharge day management service can be split/shared between the Non-Physician Practitioner (NPP) and physician. When the service is shared between a physician and an NPP from the same group practice and the physician provides any face-to-face portion of the E/M encounter with the patient, the service may be billed under either the physician's or the NPP's UPIN/PIN number.

If there was no face-to-face encounter between the patient and the physician (e.g., even if the physician participated in the service by only reviewing the patient's medical record) then the service may only be billed under the Non Physician Practitioner's NPI/PIN..

Medicare will pay for pronouncement of death as long as the provider actually does the pronouncement face-to-face with the deceased patient (not over the telephone). There must be documentation supporting a face-to-face encounter when billing a discharge service on the date of death. If the provider does not see the patient prior to the time of death or make the pronouncement of death face-to-face, no E/M service may be billed for that date of service.

## Modifiers

Modifiers will make a difference on whether you're paid on a claim and even how much you're paid on a claim. Modifiers are either created or owned by the American Medical Association (2 digit numeral modifiers) or the Centers for Medicare & Medicaid Services (CMS) which are usually alpha numeric modifiers.

While there are dozens (if not hundreds) of modifiers, we'll only discuss a few that most physicians should be familiar with as they are used pretty routinely.

Some claims may only require one modifier on a procedure code, while some instances may necessitate two modifiers on a procedure code. it all depends on the circumstances.

## Modifier 24

Modifier 24 is used on an E&M service to denote the visit is Unrelated E/M service by the same physician during a post operative period, by the same physician. Knowing that many procedures have a global fee period, the physician and staff should be aware of what those global fee periods are. You can download the most current listing of the Medicare global fee periods at **www.donself.com** in Excel or PDF format. So, you use this modifier to show that today's visit is NOT related to a global fee period of a previous procedure that YOU (or someone else with your DNA in your practice) performed. It doesn't matter if a surgeon across town or even across the street did a procedure a week ago, as their global fee period does not extend to you (assuming they have different DNA), but the services you have done may affect today's services.

As an example, a week ago, a patient was in your office and you destroyed some premalignant lesions on the patient's arm (17000 & 17003). Today, the patient is back in to see you for a headache after listening to the news that Obama raised taxes again.

If you billed today's office visit without a modifier, it would be denied by Medicare or other carriers following Medicare's Global Fee Periods – since it was less than 10 days since the procedure (since code 17000 has a 10 day global).

It doesn't matter that the diagnosis codes clearly indicate that one is not related to the other as the computers at the insurance carrier is not programmed for that distinction.    Therefore, you would need to use the modifier 24 on today's E&M visit.

# Modifier 25

Modifier 25 denotes the E&M service is significant and separately identifiable from a procedure performed on the same date, by the same physician.    Both the medically necessary E/M service and the procedure must be appropriately and sufficiently documented by the physician or midlevel in the patient's medical record to support the claim for the E&M service.

Different diagnoses are not required by Medicare for reporting the E/M service on the same date as the procedure or other service. Modifier -25 is added to the E/M code on the claim.

Originally, you did not need a modifier 25 on a visit code unless the procedure being performed on the same date was assigned a 1 or 10 day global fee period, but that has changed.   The National Correct Coding Initiative edits have now required you use the modifier 25 for a visit to show it is significant and separately identifiable if you bill many other procedures with a visit code, even if the procedure has no global fee period.   Therefore, you should always check the most current NCCI edit listing before filing claims.   You can download the most current

NCCI listing for free, from CMS at: http://www.cms.hhs.gov/NationalCorrectCodInitEd/NCCIEP/list.asp The codes in the first column bundle the codes in the second column. You may wish to download the most current listings in Excel so that you can review them anytime you wish to, without having to access the internet.

Modifier 25 should NOT be used routinely, just to get something paid, unless the visit and the documentation clearly shows that the visit was significant and separately identifiable, since many procedures include a certain amount of pre and post procedure evaluation and management services. For instance, let's assume a patient presents with back pain, stiff joints, and a headache to your Osteopathic office. Your doctor would get a history and an exam and make the medical decision making to perform an OMT (Osteopathic Manipulation Treatment), which has a 1 day global fee period.

Your doctor may bill any one of the five OMT codes (98925-98929) and an office visit with a 25 modifier because the history, exam and mdm were medically indicated and significant enough to warrant a visit.

Many times, with patients with Somatic Dysfunction, the physician may need to bring the patient back a few days later for a second treatment to achieve the desired results. Although we charged a visit (with a modifier 25) and an OMT today, when the patient comes back in, there is NOT the medical necessity to get a new history, a new exam and a new medical decision making beyond that which is normally bundled into the OMT, so no visit should be billed that day (in most cases).

Naturally, if the patient does what so few patients do – during the visit – which is "By the way, doctor – while I'm here, I get up and go pee pee 6 times a night, every night. Is that normal?", then you may very well have an office visit justifiable for today – again with a 25 modifier. Every visit needs to be weighed individually to see whether the modifier is appropriate or not.

You do not want to get into the habit, as a billing agent, claims clerk, etc... of just adding the 25 modifier to claims without knowing that it is truly justified.

If you do, you may be responsible for not only the physician having to wear an orange jumpsuit to pick up trash on the side of the highway, but you yourself having to put in a change of address at the post office to redirect your personal mail to a federal institution. Even though it may be YOUR decision to use a modifier or code, it will be you AND the physician paying for it.

This is an area that will be looked at by the Recovery Audit Contractors, Office of Inspector General, Blue Cross auditors, Coast Guard, and everyone else – so don't use it if it isn't documented and appropriate.

## Modifier 52 Vs Modifier 53

Modifier 52 denotes "reduced services", while modifier 53 denotes "discontinued services". Modifier 52 usually reduces the payment by the payer at much less than does Modifier 53.

You would use modifier 52 on a code, such as, 15851 (Removal of Sutures under general anesthesia, other than surgeon) if you removed sutures in your office without using anesthesia.

Many carriers will pay you more than $120 for this. We do recommend you add "no anesthesia rendered" in block 19 on the claim, so that the carrier can see why you have used the 52.

You would use modifier 53 on a code, such as, 45331 (Diagnostic Sigmoidoscopy) if you attempted the sigmoidoscopy but could not complete it due the patient either not being prepared properly or complaining of pain when you inserted the scope.

There appears to be quite a bit of confusion as to when a practice should use modifier 52 instead of 53 or vice-versa.

## Modifier 52:

Reduced Services: Under certain circumstances, a service or procedure is partially reduced or eliminated at the physician's discretion. Under these circumstances, the service provided can be identified by its usual procedure number and the addition of the modifier '52', signifying that the service is reduced. This provides a means of reporting reduced services without disturbing the identification of the basic service. This also means that the physician is not doing all of what the CPT code designates.

## Modifier 53:

Discontinued Procedure: Under certain circumstances, the physician may elect to terminate a surgical or diagnostic procedure. Due to extenuating circumstances or those that threaten the well being of the patient, it may be necessary to indicate that a surgical or diagnostic procedure was started but discontinued.
This modifier is not used to report the elective cancellation of a procedure prior to the patient's anesthesia induction and/or surgical preparation in the operating suite.
You CANNOT use either of these with a patient that doesn't show up for the service. You also cannot use 53 unless the procedure or anesthesia has been initiated. Initiated does not mean that the nurses have obtained the vitals.

## Modifier 59

Modifier 59 indicates "Distinct Procedural Service and should be used on procedures and not usually on E&M services. There will be times when the physician or provider may need to indicate that a procedure or service was distinct or independent from other procedures performed on the same day and not bundled into or a part of the other procedure. Modifier 59 is used to identify procedures/services that are not normally reported together, but are appropriate under the circumstances. This may represent a different session or patient encounter, different procedure or surgery, different site or organ system, separate incision/excision, separate lesion, or separate injury (or area of injury in extensive injuries)not ordinarily encountered or performed on the same day by the same physician. Many will tell you to use the modifier 59 on the SECOND procedure.

I've seen too many instances when the carrier bundled the first procedure into the second one, improperly, so we've adopted the policy of placing it on both procedures to show they are both distinct from each other.

As an example, let's say you have an office visit and a removal of impacted cerumen billed. You would not need the modifier 59 in this instance since the visit is the only other item on the claim with the removal code (69210). On the other hand, if you were also doing a destruction of premalignant lesion during the same visit, you want to make sure that the moronic insurance carrier would not bundle one distinct procedure into the other, you would use a 59 modifier on both.

You should NOT take a procedure code and unbundle it into separate components and bill each one while appending a modifier 59 as that would be considered to be unbundling, which is very illegal, unethical and ill advised. Doing so will rightfully land you in a large building, with limited views and shower facilities not affording you privacy.

Use of the modifier -59 to indicate different procedures/surgeries does not require a different diagnosis for each HCPCS/CPT coded procedure/surgery. Additionally, different diagnoses are not adequate criteria for use of modifier -59.

The HCPCS/CPT codes remain bundled unless the procedures/surgeries are performed at different anatomic sites or separate patient encounters

There are many other modifiers that physicians will use, but this will get you started on the ones that you will probably use most often.

## Progress Note Blunders
**These came out of actual progress notes:**

- By the time he was admitted, his rapid heart had stopped, and he was feeling better.
- Patient has chest pain if she lies on her left side for over a year.
- On the second day the knee was better and on the third day it had completely disappeared.
- She has had no rigors or shaking chills, but her husband states she was very hot in bed last night.
- The patient has been depressed ever since she began seeing me in 1983
- Patient was released to outpatient department without dressing.
- I have suggested that he loosen his pants before standing, and then, when he stands with the help of his wife, they should fall to the floor.
- The patient is tearful and crying constantly. She also appears to be depressed.
- The patient will need disposition, and therefore we will get Dr. Blank to dispose of him.

- The patient's past medical history has been remarkably insignificant with only a 40 pound weight gain in the past three days.
- The baby was delivered, the cord clamped & cut & handed to the pediatrician, who breathed & cried immediately
- Patient has two teenage children, but no other abnormalities
- He had a left-toe amputation one month ago. He also had a left-knee amputation last year.
- She is numb from her toes down.
- Both breasts are equal & reactive to light & accommodation.

## Signed, But Not Read

Recently, we were doing an audit in a physician's office and noticed the statement "Signed but not read" on some of the doctor's transcribed progress notes. I asked the doctor about this and he said he "didn't have time to read the typed notes and assumed they were correct".

This started me wondering about CMS' requirements for signatures on progress notes. The E&M guidelines speak about authenticating but have no requirements listed. I believe JCHO has certain requirements for hospital sites of service. Medicare also has some signature requirements of ordering diagnostic tests, but not progress notes.

A friend of mine named Quin gave a good example of what you might expect in a courtroom when a physician has used the "signed by not read" statement:

It goes something like this:

*"Are these your records Dr.?    Yes!*
*"And they contain a record of all treatment given to my*
*client?    Of course, that's what medical records are?"*
*"Could you explain to the judge just what you did when*
*you treated the flimflam and exercised the bo didly?*
*Uhhhh"*

Of course, I'm going to strongly recommend you contact your malpractice carrier and ask them what they recommend.

## Sports & School Physicals

The answer of how to bill for sports physicals depends on whom you ask. Some people promote the idea of using preventive medicine codes while others like the idea of using office visit codes 99201 – 99215. The debate will rage as to whether the annual preventive code is much more comprehensive than the routine "Can I play baseball on my school team?" exam, or what code do we use to FORCE the insurance carrier to cover something they said they don't want to cover.

We do not EVER believe you should be billing the insurance carrier for a simple sports physical, as NONE of the CPT codes describes this brief, non-illness-related visit. We recommend you make the patient's family pay cash for the visit and if they want a receipt with a code on it – use the code SPORT (five digits so it will fit in your computer system  and collect the cash. If it falls into the other categories shown above – use one of those codes.

# Health Reform

At the time this book was being written the Congress of the United States & the President of the USofA (Obama) have been "reforming" the health care and the health care industry in this country into what many (including myself) consider socialized medicine.  It is my belief that the end result will be higher unemployment, high insurance premiums and a higher taxes on all Americans (not just the rich, as the left keeps saying). Time will tell whether I am right or wrong.

As a consequence, there is quite a bit of fear in the general public today about the future of the USofA's economy, healthcare, employment and business environment.  A lot of people are scared.  A poll this past week reported that more than 70% of Americans fear an economic collapse in this country and patients with Medicare Advantage plans are scared that they will lose their coverage within the next 2 years.

Physicians are scared, and some of them have a right to be.  Others, such as primary care, should not be.  In fact, the only ones that it looks like will benefit from the Obamacare Health Reform will be the primary care physicians.  Regardless if the Health Reform that was passed in March 2010 is held to be unconstitutional in the federal courts or the U.S. Supreme Court, physicians should realize that Evidenced Based Medicine is here and it's here to stay.

Only someone with their head in the sand (or someplace else) could not see that Evidenced Based Medicine is not only helping to achieve better medical outcomes, but it is saving $ Billions to the insurance carriers, payers and programs like Medicare, Medicaid and Tricare.

The problem is tying to get hard headed, know-it-all physicians to realize that the way they have been practicing for 15 to 20 years may not be the BEST way to practice. It's similar to the man who walks into his kitchen and sees his wife cooking as she cuts the end off of a ham and places the ham in the pan and slides it into the oven, He walks over and picks up the end piece and asks her why she cut the end off and is told "I don't know – but my mom taught me how to cook and that's how I've always done it".

His mother-in-law happens to be visiting, so he asks her and is told the same answer: ""I don't know – but my mom taught me how to cook and that's how I've always done it" So – he picks up the phone and calls his wife's grandmother and asks her the same question.

After a moment of silence, the grandmother starts laughing and answers: "You know, I haven't done that since 1962 when Poppa bought me the bigger cookware"

The problem is that many of your reading this book have been cutting the end off your ham for so long, you have NO idea why you do it – but you keep doing it. That could be how you handle adjustments on your accounts receivable or how you sign patients in or if could be how the physician practices. Just because it has been done a certain way for a long time – that doesn't mean it's the best way. How long did doctors NOT wash their hands? How many patients died as a result of "bleeding" the patients? Your physicians have a choice. Continue doing what you've always done and get the same results you've always gotten – or follow Evidenced Based Medicine and see why tens of thousands of physicians are getting better results with their patients than you're getting with yours.

If your wife or husband was going to a doctor – would you rather they go to someone still doing things the same way for the past 15 years or someone who was getting better results by following the gold standards set down by the American College of Cardiology, American Association of Clinical Endocrinologists, the American Academy of Family Practice, etc...

Personally, I've met a lot of doctors that I would NOT send my family member to because they were NOT doing point of care testing and they were waiting until a problem was systematic before they would capture the problem.   By then – it might be too late to intervene successfully.   That is why I've helped thousands of physicians switch over to Evidenced Based Medicine in my seminars, webinars & consulting with Keith.

Physicians that are NOT following Evidenced Based Medicine guidelines, such as PQRI or AHRQ will lose patients to those that are.  Insurance carriers will soon figure out which physicians have chosen to continue giving mediocre care and which ones are getting better results and they WILL steer patients to those achieving better outcomes.  That's simply good business on their part and the government will be doing the same thing. If you wait until then to start doing it, it may be too late.

Along the same lines, it's also time to take your head out of the sand when it comes to ERISA. I'm already working on a book about ERISA as the Employee Retirement Income Security Act of 1974 affects EVERY person reading this book. Every one! More than 80% of the non government claims you're filing deals with ERISA and if Obama's plan stands as constitutional, then that number will probably extend to about 93% of the claims and ERISA will help you – but only if you learn it.

In the meantime, until I get my book about ERISA written, I recommend you check out what Dr. Jin Zhou at www.erisaclaim.com has to say. I also recommend the seminars and writings of Steve Verno on the ERISA issues as he has a way of simplifying it.

## Future Plans

After running an informal and non scientific survey, I discovered that a majority of people would like me to publish several books on different subjects rather than try to compete with War And Peace in size, trying to get it all into the same binding. I don't know if this has anything to do with the number of hernias and back injuries they may experience in carrying a monstrosity or not.

So, this is the first of several books that will be titled Don's Unfiltered Guide to ... I've also been approached by a publishing company that publishes text books for colleges and professional schools for medical office personnel about creating a text book with lesson plans, tests, study guides, etc, so that is also in the plans.

There is so much to teach about improving the diagnostics and clinical lab in primary care offices, that you can bet that one of the books will be about that subject specifically and another one solely on ERISA. ERISA has so many ramifications and less than 2% of the medical offices today have ANY idea of how much it can benefit them, so that is definitely on the horizon.

## Offer From The Author

If you are in a Family Practice, Internal Medicine or Geriatric Practice in the United States, the author will be glad to spend an hour on the phone with you, as long as the physician and the office manager are on the call, asking questions about your particular practice. We'll ask about your patient flow, patient mix, insurance mix, diagnosis mix, services you provide, which ones you send out, and more. We'll ask about specific coding areas, common procedures performed and how they are billed and which clinical lab you're performing in house and which ones you're referring out.

At the end of the call, we'll make specific recommendations for your practice to help you fall in line with Evidenced Based Medicine guidelines. We will also give you ideas of what you need to do to increase your income or identify areas where you may be flagging audits or committing insurance or coding abuse or fraud. All of this for free for offices that have purchased this book. If you're interested, send an email to donself@donself.com.

Please let me know at **www.donself.com** what subjects you want future books on or if you want to order an E&M Documentation sliderule described in this book, and thank YOU!

"Complete practice management, authoritative and experienced writings are difficult to come by. Don's book is one that qualifies. All in healthcare management should read it." Terry McVey, President, McVey Associates, Inc.

*"The Unfiltered Guide To Medical Office Management"* written by Don Self will keep you interested, give you knowledge and make you laugh at the same time. I have read many practice management books over the past 9 years and this book is a keeper. I would advise any practice manager to make this small investment for their career. Desiree R. Baylin, CMOM, CPM-HRS    Exec. Dir. Physician Office Managers Association of America (POMAA)

Along with their diploma, this book should be given to all medical school graduates. I only wish we had this type of practical information available when my husband started his practice! Marvel J Hammer RN CPC CCS-P PCS ACS-PM CHCO    MJH Consulting